100 MUST-READ

HISTORICAL
NOVELS

Nick Rennison

A & C Black • London

First published 2009

A & C Black Publishers Limited
36 Soho Square
London W1D 3QY
www.acblack.com

Copyright © Nick Rennison 2009

Nick Rennison has asserted his rights under the Copyright, Designs
and Patents Act, 1988, to be identified as the author of this work

A CIP catalogue record for this book is available from the
British Library.

ISBN: 978 1 408 11396 7

Typeset in 8.5pt on 12pt Meta-Light

Printed in the UK by CPI Bookmarque, Croydon, CR0 4TD

This book is produced using paper that is made from wood
grown in managed, sustainable forests. It is natural, renewable
and recyclable. The logging and manufacturing processes conform
to the environmental regulations of the country of origin.

CONTENTS

ABOUT THIS BOOK

This book is not intended to provide a list of the one hundred 'best' historical novels ever published. Given the sheer range of such fiction and the unpredictability of individual taste, any such definitive list is an impossibility. Instead I have chosen one hundred books to read which I think will provide some sense of the enormous range of novels – from an eight hundred-page volume purporting to be the memoirs of Cleopatra to a series of vignettes of English village life through the centuries, from a detective story set in medieval Shrewsbury to a portrait of a nineteenth-century Sicilian nobleman – which can be classified as 'historical fiction'.

The individual entries in the guide are arranged A to Z by author. They describe the chosen books as concisely as possible (while aiming to avoid too many 'spoilers') and say something briefly about the writer and his or her life and career. Significant film versions of the books (with dates of release) are noted where applicable, followed by 'Read On' lists comprising books by the same author, books by stylistically similar writers or books on a theme relevant to the main entry. Scattered throughout the text there are also 'Read on a Theme' menus which list between six and a dozen titles united by a common theme. The symbol

>> before an author name indicates that the author is one of those covered in the A to Z entries.

How far back in the past does a book have to be set in order to qualify as a 'historical' novel? Is *The Rotters' Club*, Jonathan Coe's wonderful story of four schoolboys growing up in 1970s Britain, a historical novel? It was written in the 1990s and therefore its setting is the past. However, it is difficult to see a novel set in so recent a past as 'historical'. There has to be some significant passage of time between the period described and the period in which the book was written. The problem then becomes one of defining the word 'significant' in this context. In the final analysis, any definition is arbitrary but I have chosen to make sixty years the significant passage of time. Mostly this was to allow myself the opportunity to include books set during the Second World War which seem to me to fall, almost indisputably, into the category of 'historical fiction'. Partly, it was because Sir Walter Scott's *Waverley*, a novel which has as good a claim as any to be the first important work of historical fiction, was subtitled ''Tis Sixty Years Since' and was set at the time of the Jacobite Rebellion, sixty years before Scott published it in 1805. I liked the coincidence between the time span I had already more or less decided upon and Scott's sub-title. This 'sixty-year rule' applies to all one hundred main choices in this guide. As a result, there are titles some readers might expect to see in a guide to historical fiction which are missing. By many definitions *War and Peace*, for example, is an historical novel. However, Tolstoy was writing about events and characters from the 1810s in the 1860s and thus falls foul of the sixty-year rule. This did seem a rather significant omission but I consoled myself with the thought that there is an entry for *War and*

Peace in *100 Must-Read Classic Novels*, one of the other books in this series, and I stuck to my rule. The vast majority of the 'read on' selections also follow the rule but I have included a few titles which fell outside it but which none the less seemed such appropriate additions to particular lists that I decided bending it was acceptable.

All the first choice books in this guide have a date attached to them. In the case of British and American writers, this date refers to the first publication in the UK or the USA. For translated writers, dates of publication refer to the book's first appearance in English.

INTRODUCTION

Some of the very first bestselling novels were historical ones. ›› Sir Walter Scott's novels, excursions through (mostly) Scottish history, were sensations of their day. The first edition of **Waverley**, a tale of Bonnie Prince Charlie's rebellion, sold a thousand copies in two days when it was published in 1814 which may not seem much when compared with Pottermania in the early twenty-first century but was considered pretty astounding at the time. Scott inspired a multitude of other writers to peer back into the past. In France, ›› Alexandre Dumas launched himself on an astonishingly prolific career which saw him raid every major event in French history from the sixteenth-century Wars of Religion to the Revolution for fictional plots. In Italy, Alessandro Manzoni openly acknowledged his debt to Scott's *Ivanhoe* when his novel *I Promessi Sposi* (*The Betrothed*) became a huge success. Over on the other side of the Atlantic, James Fenimore Cooper swapped Scott's kilts for leatherstockings and wrote *The Deerslayer* and *The Last of the Mohicans*, in which rugged pioneers in eighteenth century America battled against nature and treacherous Indians to push the frontier forwards.

Throughout the nineteenth century, historical novels continued to be bestsellers. Edward Bulwer Lytton travelled back to Roman times for *The Last Days of Pompeii*. Captain Marryat pioneered the nautical-historical fiction which still has plenty of practitioners today and, in 1847, also published *The Children of the New Forest*, set in the English Civil War and familiar to generations of young English readers. Harrison Ainsworth is more or less forgotten today but, in the 1840s, he was nearly as popular as ›› Dickens and he owed his reputation to a string of historical novels. Dick Turpin, the highwayman, would not be the figure of legend and romance he still is if he had not appeared as a leading character in Ainsworth's 1839 novel *Rookwood*. Dickens himself journeyed back in time for *A Tale of Two Cities* and *Barnaby Rudge* and most of the great novelists of the Victorian era, from Thackeray (*The History of Henry Esmond*) to ›› George Eliot (*Romola*) ventured into the past for at least one of their plots. In France, ›› Victor Hugo, in *Notre-Dame de Paris*, introduced the world's most famous fictional hunchback in Quasimodo in a tale of fifteenth-century Paris.

In America, by the last decades of the nineteenth century, the historical novel was firmly established as a bestselling genre. When the Civil War general ›› Lew Wallace decided to try his hand at fiction, he turned to the past and wrote *Ben-Hur*. The mix of chariot-racing and early Christianity proved a powerful one and the book was a huge success. The template Wallace created was still being used sixty years later. *The Robe* and *The Big Fisherman*, bestselling novels of the 1940s written by a Lutheran minister named Lloyd C. Douglas, employed the same technique of combining the life of Christ with rip-roaring adventure and heart-tugging pathos. *The Robe*, although it is now remembered only for its movie version, the first film in Cinemascope, sold more than two million copies in the US.

At the same time as Wallace was turning his imagination towards the Roman Empire a huge market for historical novels for boys developed in Britain, partly as a result of the increased literacy that followed the expansion and improvement of the educational system. These usually focused on heroes whose manly exploits demonstrated the virtues of empire. The most famous exponent of this kind of fiction was G.A. Henty and titles from his lengthy bibliography such as *With Clive in India*, *St George for England* and *Under Drake's Flag* indicate pretty clearly the kind of books they were.

It wasn't just in the realms of juvenile fiction that history held sway. In the late Victorian and Edwardian eras, historical fiction attracted attention and kudos. ❯❯ Sir Arthur Conan Doyle famously longed for recognition as a historical novelist rather than as the creator of Sherlock Holmes. *The White Company* and *Sir Nigel*, two books featuring manly English soldiers valiantly smiting the French during the Hundred Years War, were labours of love, although they would probably be entirely forgotten today if their author had not also been the man who gave us the great detective. Some writers in the first decades of the twentieth century built entire, bestselling careers on their historical fiction. Doyle's younger contemporaries Jeffery Farnol and ❯❯ Rafael Sabatini published their first novels in the Edwardian era and both were still writing tales of swashbuckling romance and derring-do in the late 1940s. Stories like *Captain Blood* and *Scaramouche* are best remembered in their film versions but a Jeffery Farnol Appreciation Society still exists and all of Sabatini's fiction can be found on the web without much difficulty. Old-fashioned these books may be but somebody still loves them.

As the twentieth century progressed, the fascination with stories from the past showed no signs of flagging. The two bestselling books in America in the 1930s were both works of historical fiction. Margaret Mitchell's *Gone with the Wind*, the story of Scarlett O'Hara and her struggle to survive the American Civil War, remains a much-loved work. By contrast, the fame of Hervey Allen's *Anthony Adverse* has largely disappeared, although, at the time, it was as familiar as Mitchell's Deep South epic. And, in Britain, a new form of historical fiction – the historical romance – was gathering popularity. The name most closely associated with the sub-genre is ➤➤ Georgette Heyer who began to publish fiction in the 1920s and went on to become almost synonymous with the 'Regency romance'. Other writers also carved out highly successful and long-lasting careers. Eleanor Hibbert (1906–93), for example, employed a series of pseudonyms that included 'Jean Plaidy', 'Victoria Holt', and 'Philippa Carr' to publish well over a hundred romantic novels set in a variety of historical eras.

Readers continue to love historical fiction today. Indeed, if anything, historical novels are more popular now than at any point since Scott first published the 'Waverley' novels. A swift survey of today's bestseller lists provides the evidence for this. Anything written by Bernard Cornwell, whether set in Napoleonic Europe or King Alfred's Britain, will climb the charts as soon as it is published. Philippa Gregory on sex, love and scandal at the Tudor court is a surefire recipe for success. The list of books chosen for Richard and Judy's Summer Reads always includes a healthy proportion of historical fiction. Critical praise as well as commercial success continues to be lavished on books set in the past. Look at the list of novels which have won or been shortlisted for the Man Booker Prize in the forty years of its existence. From ➤➤ J.G. Farrell's *The Siege of Krishnapur* to ➤➤ William Golding's *Rites of Passage*, from ➤➤ Barry Unsworth's *Sacred Hunger* to ➤➤ Pat Barker's *The Ghost Road*, many of the books that have caught the judges' eyes have been historical novels. The genre is thriving today as much as it has ever done.

A–Z LIST OF ENTRIES BY AUTHOR

Charles Dickens	*A Tale of Two Cities*
E.L. Doctorow	*Ragtime*
Sir Arthur Conan Doyle	*The White Company*
Alexandre Dumas	*The Three Musketeers*
Daphne Du Maurier	*Jamaica Inn*
Dorothy Dunnett	*Niccolo Rising*
Umberto Eco	*The Name of the Rose*
Robert Edric	*The Book of the Heathen*
Thomas Eidson	*St Agnes' Stand*
George Eliot	*Romola*
Michel Faber	*The Crimson Petal and the White*
J.G. Farrell	*The Siege of Krishnapur*
Patricia Finney	*Firedrake's Eye*
Penelope Fitzgerald	*The Blue Flower*
Ken Follett	*The Pillars of the Earth*
Ford Madox Ford	*The Fifth Queen*
C.S. Forester	*The Happy Return*
John Fowles	*The French Lieutenant's Woman*
George MacDonald Fraser	*Flashman*
Charles Frazier	*Cold Mountain*
Margaret George	*The Memoirs of Cleopatra*
William Golding	*Rites of Passage*
Robert Graves	*I, Claudius*
Philippa Gregory	*The Queen's Fool*
Kate Grenville	*The Secret River*
Robert Harris	*Pompeii*
Georgette Heyer	*A Civil Contract*
Peter Ho Davies	*The Welsh Girl*

Steven Pressfield	*Gates of Fire*
Julian Rathbone	*The Last English King*
Mary Renault	*The Praise Singer*
Derek Robinson	*Goshawk Squadron*
Jane Rogers	*Mr Wroe's Virgins*
Rafael Sabatini	*Captain Blood*
C.J. Sansom	*Dissolution*
Steven Saylor	*Roman Blood*
Sir Walter Scott	*Rob Roy*
Anya Seton	*Katherine*
Michael Shaara	*The Killer Angels*
Jane Smiley	*The All-true Travels and Adventures of Lidie Newton*
Robert Louis Stevenson	*Kidnapped*
Patrick Süskind	*Perfume*
Rosemary Sutcliff	*The Eagle of the Ninth*
Andrew Taylor	*The American Boy*
Adam Thorpe	*Ulverton*
Rose Tremain	*Restoration*
Barry Unsworth	*Morality Play*
Guy Vanderhaeghe	*The Last Crossing*
Gore Vidal	*Burr*
Lew Wallace	*Ben-Hur*
Mika Waltari	*The Egyptian*
Sarah Waters	*Fingersmith*
Patrick White	*Voss*
Marguerite Yourcenar	*Memoirs of Hadrian*
Richard Zimler	*The Last Kabbalist of Lisbon*

A–Z OF ENTRIES

PETER ACKROYD (b. 1949) UK

DAN LENO AND THE LIMEHOUSE GOLEM (1994)

All of Peter Ackroyd's work – as novelist, biographer, historian and critic – is linked by two preoccupations. One is his fascination with London, the city of his birth. The other is his belief in the intimate connections between past and present. In *Hawksmoor*, first published in 1985 and still his most original novel, a contemporary detective (the namesake of the eighteenth century architect) moves towards a mystical encounter with forces from the past as he investigates a series of murders in London churches. In *Chatterton* three different narratives, one from the eighteenth century, one from the Victorian era and one from the present day, intertwine and interact. Both these books are, in a sense, historical novels but much of their power derives from the tension between a contemporary London story and ones from the city's history. Ackroyd has also written fiction which is set exclusively in the past. *Dan Leno and the Limehouse Golem*, for example, evokes the world of late-Victorian music-hall and focuses, like *Hawksmoor*, on a series of killings. Real individuals like Karl Marx and the novelist George Gissing interact with the author's inventions; fable and murder mystery mix with Gothic comedy; different narrative voices combine and contend in a way characteristic of Ackroyd's fiction. The novel opens with the hanging of Elizabeth Cree for the poisoning of her husband, John. From there it moves backwards in time to reconstruct Elizabeth's life from poverty-blighted childhood in Lambeth through a career in the music hall (where she works with the famous Dan Leno) to her eventual execution. In parallel with Elizabeth's story, the novel follows a sequence of brutal murders which are attributed to a bogeyman named the Limehouse Golem. As various threads of the narrative intertwine, possible connections between the story of Elizabeth and that of the Golem are gradually glimpsed. Throughout this unsettling story of Victorian London, Ackroyd's exceptional skill both in evoking the past and manipulating the expectations of his readers is much in evidence.

🥢 Read on
Chatterton; *Hawksmoor*; *The Lambs of London*
John Boyne, *Crippen*; Peter Carey, *Jack Maggs*

MARGARET ATWOOD (b. 1939) CANADA

ALIAS GRACE (1996)
Poet and short story-writer as well as novelist, Margaret Atwood is one of the most gifted of contemporary writers and her fiction has ranged from the dazzling dystopia of *The Handmaid's Tale* to the sexual power games of *Life Before Man*. *Alias Grace*, one of her finest works of

fiction, is an exploration of women's sexuality and social roles wrapped up in a gripping story of a nineteenth-century housemaid who may or may not have been a murderess. It takes a notorious case from Canada's past and re-imagines it. When the novel begins, the year is 1851 and, in Kingston penitentiary, Ontario, Grace Marks is serving a prison sentence for her involvement in the murders, some years earlier, of her employer and his housekeeper. She has always claimed to have no memories of these murders. Some people believe her to be innocent and they have asked a young doctor with a growing reputation in psychological medicine, Simon Jordan, to interview her. Through the medium of the (fictional) Jordan, we hear the story of Grace's life from the arrival of her family in Canada as enforced exiles from poverty-stricken Ireland to the events leading up to the murder. The doctor endeavours to use his knowledge of the burgeoning science of psychology to unlock the mystery of Grace's personality but the uneducated servant-girl proves more than a match for him. Atwood has written that, 'the true character of the historical Grace Marks remains an enigma' and the same can be said of the fictional version of Grace that the novelist has created. *Alias Grace* is a novel that raises more questions than it answers but that becomes one of its many strengths. Refusing to accept simplistic explanations of what might have happened and what Grace's motivations might have been, Atwood creates a complex and ambivalent portrait of a young woman trapped by poverty and the expectations of the society in which she lives.

⮐ Read on

The Blind Assassin
Toni Morrison, *Beloved*; Barbara Kingsolver, *The Poisonwood Bible*

BERYL BAINBRIDGE (b. 1934) UK

MASTER GEORGIE (1998)

Beryl Bainbridge began her career as a novelist with books in which she drew upon her own upbringing in Liverpool and her personal experience to create blackly comic narratives that placed the mundane and the unsettling side by side on the page. In the last twenty years she has turned more frequently to the past for her subjects and she has written books which provide her own off-beat and oblique views of iconic events and individuals in English history, from the sinking of the Titanic to the Crimean War, from Captain Scott to Dr Johnson. As a historical novelist, Bainbridge is a miniaturist and she shies away from the epic and the grandiose. This is clear from *Master Georgie*, the novel set in the Crimean War. The most famous events and people of the war play little part in Bainbridge's story. The Charge of the Light Brigade merits one brief reference so throwaway it is easily missed. The Lady with the Lamp is conspicuous by her absence. Instead the emphasis is on one small group of Liverpudlians. George Hardy is a prosperous surgeon from the city and an enthusiast for the new art of photography. Volunteering to take his medical skills to the Crimea, he is accompanied there by an eccentric entourage of friends and family, including Myrtle, his adoring adoptive sister, Dr Potter, his increasingly troubled brother-in-law, and an ex-street urchin named Pompey Jones who has a mysterious hold over Master Georgie. Structured around the notion of six photographic plates and told in the voices of several of the characters, the novel chronicles the party's disintegration in the face of the death and disease they find in the war zone and the gradual emergence of hidden truths about their personal and erotic entanglements.

☛ Read on
Every Man for Himself; *Young Adolf*
J.L. Carr, *A Month in the Country*; ›› Penelope Fitzgerald, *The Beginning of Spring*

JOHN BANVILLE (b. 1945) IRELAND

DOCTOR COPERNICUS (1976)

As a young writer John Banville published a collection of short stories and two novels which were well received in his native Ireland and, in his early thirties, he embarked on an ambitious sequence of books focused on scientific geniuses of the past – a sequence sometimes known as 'The Revolutions Trilogy'. *Doctor Copernicus* (1976) brings to life the Polish/German priest whose theories undermined medieval ideas about man's position in the universe. It was followed by *Kepler* (1981) and *The Newton Letter* (1982), a story largely set in contemporary Ireland but with a central character obsessed by writing a biography of Isaac Newton. All the books show Banville's ability to weave together a compelling narrative with intellectual speculation and playfulness. His Copernicus is a man haunted by doubts about the value of his new heliocentric ideas and neurotically unwilling to commit them to the finality of publication. We are used to the idea of writers, painters and composers suffering for their art in fiction but Banville offers the much less common sight of the anguished scientist. His Copernicus is a passive and introverted figure whose only real moments of joy come though intellectual insight when it feels 'as if the channels of his brain had been sluiced with an icy drench of water'. However, Banville succeeds in bringing this rather cold and unsympathetic man to life. His vacillation and his agonised uncertainty about the ability he, or anyone else, possesses to understand God's universe are made real. His doubt becomes moving and poignant. In recent years, Banville's fiction has attracted ever greater plaudits, culminating in the award of the Man Booker prize for his 2005 novel *The Sea*, but there is a case to be made that his best work can still be found in the historical fiction he published much earlier in his career.

🐢 **Read on**
Kepler
Daniel Kehlmann, *Measuring the World*; Alan Lightman, *Einstein's Dreams*

PAT BARKER (b. 1943) UK

REGENERATION (1990)

Pat Barker had written a number of novels which turned an unsentimental eye on working-class life in her native Teesside, particularly the life led by working-class women, before she achieved a critical and commercial breakthrough with *Regeneration*, a novel which tapped into the deep-rooted and continuing fascination the British have with the events of the First World War. *Regeneration* is the first book in a trilogy of novels which tells the story of Billy Prior, a working-class bisexual soldier of the Great War, and his experiences in the trenches and at the Craiglockhart War Hospital which, under its chief psychotherapist, William Rivers, specialises in the treatment of the newly categorised mental illness known as 'shell shock'. Throughout the trilogy Barker skilfully mixes together wholly fictional characters like Prior and her own versions of real people such as Rivers and the poets Siegfried Sassoon and Wilfred Owen, both of whom were patients at the hospital. The first of the novels is set at Craiglockhart in 1917. Sassoon, a war hero, has made a public statement condemning the unnecessary prolongation of the war and, rather than face the embarrassment of court-martialling a decorated and well-known officer, the army has packed him off to the hospital for treatment. Much of the book focuses on the interaction of Sassoon and Rivers, the 'disturbed' soldier who appears only too clear-sightedly sane and the therapist whose role is, ultimately, to ready him for a return to the insanity of the front line. Meanwhile Billy Prior, who has been rendered mute by his terrible experiences in the trenches and can communicate with Rivers only through writing on a pad, is able to make some reconnection with the world through his relationship with Sarah Lumb, a young woman whose boyfriend has been killed in the war. *Regeneration* and the two novels which follow it – complex narratives which explore ideas of masculinity, sexuality, class and madness with great subtlety – form the most persuasive investigation of the First World War and what it meant to the British in recent fiction.

🎞 **Film version:** *Regeneration* (1997, with James Wilby as Sassoon and Jonathan Pryce as Rivers)

📖 **Read on**
The Eye in the Door; *The Ghost Road* (the other two volumes in the trilogy)
Sebastian Barry, *A Long, Long Way*; Sebastian Faulks, *Birdsong*

READONATHEME: THE FIRST WORLD WAR AND ITS AFTERMATH

Helen Dunmore, *Zennor in Darkness*
Ben Elton, *The First Casualty*
Timothy Findley, *The Wars*
Susan Hill, *Strange Meeting*
Sebastien Japrisot, *A Very Long Engagement*
Deborah Moggach, *In the Dark* (the Home Front during World War I)
Michael Morpurgo, *Private Peaceful* (a children's book but one which adults will also find moving and rewarding)
Jeff Shaara, *To the Last Man*
Charles Todd, *A Test of Wills*

ANDREA BARRETT (b. 1954) USA

THE VOYAGE OF THE NARWHAL (1998)

The year is 1855. Some years earlier, the famous British explorer Sir John Franklin and his men disappeared on a journey to the Arctic in search of the elusive North-West Passage. Fame and fortune await any man who discovers what has happened to the expedition. The handsome and charismatic Zeke Voorhees, commander of the *Narwhal*, is determined to be that man. Sailing with him is the man who is to be his brother-in-law, Erasmus Darwin Wells, a self-doubting naturalist approaching middle age who has one disastrous expedition into the ice behind him and is looking for redemption from what he sees as his previous failures. Erasmus soon begins to suspect that Zeke is not the man to provide the opportunity for it. His brother-in-law, blinded by his ambition and paranoia, puts the lives of his men at risk with his folly and recklessness. When Zeke disappears on a mad solo mission into the unknown, Erasmus is forced to make a decision on the future of the expedition which will haunt him for the rest of his life. Meanwhile, back at home, his sister Lavinia and her companion Alexandra must learn to cope with the men's absence and with the psychological pressures that brings. Andrea Barrett began to publish her fiction in the 1980s and has since gained a considerable reputation as both novelist and short-story writer. *Servants of the Map*, her collection of two novellas and four stories, the majority of which were set in the past, was shortlisted for the Pulitzer Prize for Fiction. Her most recent novel, *The Air We Breathe*, which takes place in an American sanatorium during World War I, also won much acclaim. However, *The Voyage of the Narwhal*, with its brilliant portraits of men and women engaged in exploration both geographical and personal, remains her most remarkable achievement.

🕮 Read on

The Air We Breathe; *Servants of the Map*

Steven Heighton, *Afterlands*; Sten Nadolny, *The Discovery of Slowness* (a novel about Franklin); Wayne Johnston, *The Navigator of New York*

THOMAS BERGER (b. 1924) USA

LITTLE BIG MAN (1964)

The narrator of *Little Big Man* is 111-year-old Jack Crabb, looking back on a long and extraordinary life caught between the two cultures of the white man and the Cheyenne. Born white but adopted into an Indian family, Crabb (or Little Big Man as he is to the Cheyenne) is able to bear witness for the peoples on both sides of the frontier. As Berger's novel progresses, his hero has tall tales to tell of all the legendary figures of the American West. He has tangled with Wyatt Earp and ridden with Wild Bill Hickok. During his time sharing the life of the Cheyenne he married and became a father but both his wife and his child were killed in a cavalry raid led by the dementedly charismatic US officer, George Armstrong Custer. Little Big Man vowed to kill Custer in revenge but the twists and turns of fate took him once again across the boundary between the world of the white man and the world of the Indian, and he found himself working as a scout for the Seventh Cavalry. As a result, the centenarian can make his most outrageous claim of all – that he was the sole white survivor of the Battle of the Little Big Horn and Custer's Last Stand. Thomas Berger is one of the most versatile and entertaining US novelists of his generation whose books range from a sequence of comic novels about an American everyman named Carlo Reinhart to a retelling of Arthurian legend (*Arthur Rex*) and an updating of the story of Robinson Crusoe (*Robert Crews*). *Little Big Man* was his third novel and remains his best-known. Picaresque and farcical yet also surprisingly moving, it is a wonderfully vivid account of the old West and one which successfully combines historical accuracy with riotous burlesque.

🎞 **Film version:** *Little Big Man* (directed by Arthur Penn and starring Dustin Hoffman as Jack Crabb)

📚 **Read on**
The Return of Little Big Man
Dee Brown, *Creek Mary's Blood*; Allan Gurganus, *Oldest Living Confederate Widow Tells All*

READ ON A THEME: THE AMERICAN WEST

Pete Dexter, *Deadwood*

Loren D. Estleman, *Billy Gashade*

Tom Franklin, *Hell at the Breech* (actually set in the Deep South in the 1890s but has all the characteristics of the best writing about the West)

A.B. Guthrie, *The Big Sky*

Oakley Hall, *Warlock*

Ron Hansen, *The Assassination of Jesse James by the Coward Robert Ford*

Elmer Kelton, *The Day the Cowboys Quit*

Cormac McCarthy, *Blood Meridian*

Larry McMurtry, *Lonesome Dove*

Robert B. Parker, *Gunman's Rhapsody*

Charles Portis, *True Grit*

Glendon Swarthout, *The Shootist*

WILLIAM BOYD (b. 1952) UK

AN ICE-CREAM WAR (1982)

Since the publication of his first novel in 1981, a black comedy that suggested he might be a writer to follow in the footsteps of Evelyn Waugh and Kingsley Amis, William Boyd has shown himself to be one of the most versatile novelists of his generation. He has twice used the form of imaginary memoirs as a means of weaving his fiction into the real fabric of twentieth century history. In *The New Confessions* an ageing movie director looks back at his life, from service in the First World War to film-making in Hollywood in its Golden Age; *Any Human Heart* is presented as the journals of a writer, Logan Mountstuart, who meets and interacts with some of the cultural giants of the last hundred years from Virginia Woolf to Ernest Hemingway. Boyd's most engaging historical fiction is, in some ways, a more straightforward work than either of these fabricated autobiographies. Set in the years of the First World War, *An Ice-Cream War* follows the twists and turns of the largely forgotten campaigns fought between armies from the British and German colonies in East Africa. Gabriel Cobb goes off to fight in the African campaigns. In his absence, his wife and his brother Felix act upon their attraction to one another and embark upon an affair but word soon comes through that Gabriel has been captured. Felix decides that there is only one honourable course open to him. He must track down his brother and redeem himself by rescuing Gabriel. In a novel that employs the black humour of Boyd's first novel on a much larger canvas, the central characters – the two brothers Cobb, Gabriel's erring wife Charis, the plantation owner Walter Smith, the German colonist turned soldier Erich von Bishop – all find their lives upturned and uprooted by historical events largely beyond their control.

⮒ Read on
Any Human Heart; *The Blue Afternoon*; *The New Confessions*
Giles Foden, *Ladysmith*; Uwe Timm, *Morenga* (novel by a German writer about an anti-colonial insurrection in South-West Africa in the decade before the First World War)

MELVYN BRAGG (b. 1939) UK

CREDO (1996)

The result of Melvyn Bragg's long-cherished ambition to tell the story of the Christianisation of the north of England in Anglo-Saxon times, *Credo* is one of the most satisfying historical novels published in the 1990s. It was not the first time that Bragg had looked to the past for his narratives. *The Hired Man*, the opening volume of his 'Cumbrian Trilogy', published at the end of the 1960s, is set in a thinly disguised version of Bragg's hometown Wigton in the decades immediately before and after the First World War. *The Maid of Buttermere* is his version of a real-life story from the beginning of the nineteenth-century – one which caught the imaginations of the Romantic poets Wordsworth and Coleridge – about an unspoiled Lakeland beauty seduced by an impostor and bigamist. *Credo*, however, travelled further back into the past and further away from the kind of fiction for which he is best-known. At the heart of the book is Bega, an Irish princess who is destined for a marriage appropriate to her status but is determined instead to preserve her virginity and serve God. Only her attraction to Padric, a young nobleman from the kingdom of Rheged in the north of England and a guest of her father, can compete with her piety. Padric returns to Rheged and Bega, in flight from proposed marriage to a brutish warlord, follows him, eventually taking sanctuary in the great abbey at Whitby. Over the seven hundred pages of his narrative, Bragg tells the story of Bega's commitment to her faith, her continuing bond with Padric, as he struggles to assert himself in the violent power politics of the time, and the spread of Christianity through the kingdoms of the North. Rooted in wide-ranging research into Dark Ages England, *Credo* is a brilliantly imaginative portrait of a woman torn between earthly and heavenly desires and the world of faith and faithlessness she inhabits.

📚 Read on
The Maid of Buttermere (set in the Lake District in the early years of the nineteenth century)
>> Bernard Cornwell, *The Last Kingdom*; Allan Massie, *The Evening of the World*

GERALDINE BROOKS (b. 1955) AUSTRALIA/USA

MARCH (2005)
Born and brought up in Australia, Geraldine Brooks moved to the USA in the early 1980s to complete a master's degree in journalism and she went on to forge a highly successful career as a foreign correspondent for *The Wall Street Journal*, covering events in trouble spots around the world from the Balkans to the Middle East. She has published three novels, all of them historical fiction to a greater or lesser degree. Her first novel, *Year of Wonders*, followed the lives of the inhabitants of a seventeenth-century Derbyshire village as they struggled to retain their humanity in the face of an epidemic of the plague. Her most recent work

of fiction, *People of the Book*, tells the story of a Hebrew manuscript, a mysterious codex known as the Sarajevo Haggadah, in its travels through history and through the world. *March*, her second novel, won the Pulitzer Prize for Fiction. It takes as its starting point Louisa May Alcott's *Little Women* but tells its story from the viewpoint not of any of the female characters but of the March girls' father, largely absent from the pages of Alcott's novel. (In both novels, Mr March is away from home and his girls because of the American Civil War.) An ardent abolitionist, he joins the Union army as a chaplain but his naïve ideas about the brotherhood of all men are soon undermined by the behaviour of the soldiers in his spiritual care. The racism and mindless brutality he witnesses shake his idealism and his body is all but broken by the physical illnesses he endures. As Brooks's narrative progresses, he is forced to find new ways of living with himself and of re-establishing contact with those who cannot begin to understand what he has experienced. *March* takes a much-loved classic and, by changing readers' perspectives, gives it an added and powerful resonance.

≷ Read on

Year of Wonders
Joan Brady, *Theory of War*; Edward P. Jones, *The Known World*

JOHN BUCHAN (1875–1940) UK

MIDWINTER (1923)

John Buchan, who combined a literary career with a life in public service which culminated in a five-year period as Governor-General of Canada, is best-known for his novels of espionage featuring the stiff upper-lipped adventurer Richard Hannay, of which the most famous is the frequently-filmed *The Thirty-Nine Steps*. Buchan was a prolific writer and he also wrote a number of historical novels, most of which focused on events in the history of his native Scotland. *Witch Wood*, for example, is a story of witchcraft and warfare in the Border Country during the seventeenth century. The most interesting and enjoyable of Buchan's historical novels is *Midwinter*, a tale of intrigue and treachery set in 1745 as Bonnie Prince Charlie is about to march southwards at the head of a Highland army. The central character is Alastair Maclean, a confidant of the Prince who has been despatched ahead of the troops on a secret mission to raise support for the Jacobite cause. On his journey Maclean comes across two extraordinary men. One is an aspiring poet and man of letters named Samuel Johnson. This is Johnson before he was transformed into the legendary figure we meet in Boswell's biography and Buchan's fictional portrait of him is affectionate and entirely convincing. The other is the mysterious 'Midwinter', a gentleman-outlaw who gives his name to the novel and represents the 'Old England' that survives the superficial changes of government and party politics. As Maclean begins to suspect that there is a traitor amongst the Jacobites and that someone is passing secrets to the government forces, he comes to need the help of both of these very different men. Working in the tradition of historical fiction that was developed by his two fellow Scots ➤➤ Scott and ➤➤ Stevenson, Buchan produced a novel that has much the same vigour and vitality that their works possessed.

🐃 Read on

The Blanket of the Dark; *Witch Wood*

D.K. Broster, *The Flight of the Heron*; Nigel Tranter, *MacGregor's Gathering*

A.S. BYATT (b. 1936) UK

POSSESSION (1990)

For more than forty years, A.S. Byatt has been publishing generous and erudite fiction, informed by her own expressed desire to write about 'the life of the mind as well as of society and the relations between people'. The most successful novel of her career, and one which won the Booker Prize in 1990, is *Possession*, a dazzlingly clever narrative which moves back and forth between past and present. Two contemporary scholars, Roland Mitchell and Maud Bailey, are researching the lives and works of two Victorian poets, Randolph Henry Ash and Christabel LaMotte. It has long been assumed that Ash was a doting and faithful husband and that LaMotte's emotional commitment was to her own sex but Mitchell and Bailey gradually unearth evidence of an illicit but all-consuming love affair between the two nineteenth-century writers. As they do so, their own rather arid emotional lives are deeply affected. They are people who have been shaped but also shackled by their devotion to literature and intellectual pursuits and, the more they chase the ghosts of Ash and LaMotte, the more they stretch the limitations they have imposed on themselves. *Possession* is not, by any means, a conventional historical novel. Not only do long sections of it take place in the present but it also makes bold use of unusual means to tell its story. It includes lengthy examples of Ash's and LaMotte's poetry (based on the work of Robert Browning and Christina Rossetti, they demonstrate Byatt's remarkable gifts as a literary ventriloquist), as well as letters and other documents that the two contemporary researchers investigate. It is through the hints and clues contained in these texts that the narrative – a remarkably compelling hybrid of detective story, romance and historical novel – largely emerges.

◀ **Film version:** *Possession* (2002, with Gwyneth Paltrow as Maud Bailey)

≋ **Read on**
Angels and Insects (two linked novellas set in the Victorian era)
Peter Carey, *Oscar and Lucinda*; Lindsay Clarke, *The Chymical Wedding* (very different in style and atmosphere to Byatt's work but also featuring parallel stories, one from the present and one from the nineteenth century); Jennifer Vanderbes, *Easter Island: A Novel*

READ ON A THEME: PAST AND PRESENT

Novels in which historical and contemporary stories meet and interact

>> Peter Ackroyd, *The House of Doctor Dee*
   Malcolm Bradbury, *To the Hermitage*
>> Tracy Chevalier, *The Virgin Blue*
   David Ebershoff, *The 19th Wife*
   Marina Fiorato, *The Glassblower of Murano*
   Michael Gruber, *The Book of Air and Shadows*
   James Robertson, *The Fanatic*
   Rebecca Stott, *Ghostwalk*
   Nigel Williams, *Witchcraft*

CALEB CARR (b. 1955) USA

THE ALIENIST (1994)

New York in the 1890s and a deranged murderer is butchering young transvestite prostitutes on the streets of the city. A task force of unconventional criminologists, led by a pioneering psychological profiler, is given the job of tracking the killer down. The book opens in 1919 with the narrator, a journalist named John Schuyler Moore, musing on the recent death of the ex-president, Theodore Roosevelt, and moves swiftly back to the year 1896 when Roosevelt, then New York Police Commissioner, faced a series of killings. The victims were poor immigrant boys forced into selling their bodies in the city's worst dives. Roosevelt invited Laszlo Kreizler, an old friend from Harvard, to investigate the killings and Kreizler put together an unlikely team to undertake the job, including Moore himself, a woman named Sara Howard, two Jewish brothers and police sergeants called Isaacson and Kreizler's street-smart teenage ward, Stevie Taggert. Through the eyes of Moore, readers follow the twists and turns of the investigation as Kreizler and his colleagues make use of what were then cutting-edge techniques in their attempts to track down the killer. Real individuals, from Roosevelt and the financier J.P. Morgan to the moralising busybody Anthony Comstock flit through the pages of Carr's narrative as it travels towards its final revelations about the killings. Caleb Carr, the son of Lucien Carr, a notorious figure in the history of the Beat movement, had only published one not-very-successful novel and a biography of the nineteenth-century American soldier-of-fortune Frederick Townsend Ward when *The Alienist* appeared and took the bestseller lists by storm. It is a book that deserves all the critical acclaim and the high paperback sales it has received. *The Alienist* succeeds brilliantly as a reconstruction of 1890s' New York, as an exploration of crime, insanity and freewill, and as a compelling, page-turning crime novel.

🍃 Read on

The Angel of Darkness; *The Italian Secretary* (a Sherlock Holmes pastiche)

Jake Arnott, *The Devil's Paintbrush*; Lawrence Goldstone, *The Anatomy of Deception*; Frank Tallis, *Mortal Mischief*; Eric Zencey, *Panama*

WILLA CATHER (1873–1947) USA

DEATH COMES FOR THE ARCHBISHOP (1927)

The novels for which Willa Cather is best known are largely set in the American Midwest she knew from her childhood, growing up in Nebraska at the end of the nineteenth century. *O Pioneers!* is the story of a Swedish immigrant family, the Bergsons, and their struggles to make a living from their prairie farmstead. Her finest and, in many ways, most characteristic novel, *My Ántonia*, has a similar setting. However, she also wrote fiction which ventured further back in time. *Shadows on the Rock*, for example, follows a resourceful young girl through a year of her life in the French settlements of seventeenth-century Quebec. *Death Comes for the Archbishop* is based on true events, and on diaries and letters of real people, and tells of two French Catholic missionaries to New Mexico in the mid-nineteenth century. Father Latour is a Jesuit serving in Ohio when the Church makes him bishop of a new diocese in territory only recently annexed by the USA and despatches him southwards. Accompanying him is his old friend and companion from their seminary in France, Father Vaillant. Cather's novel is not a conventional narrative but a series of vignettes which illuminate the lives and work of the two men over decades. Father Latour, on a journey with an Indian guide, spends a night sheltering in a cavern that is sacred to the native population and witnesses the continuing devotion of his nominally Christian companion to older religious traditions. He and his fellow priest assist in the rescue of a young woman from an abusive relationship and she becomes their housekeeper. The bishop's dreams of building a cathedral in Santa Fe are eventually fulfilled. Father Vaillant leaves to minister to the needs of gold rush miners. Slowly and subtly Cather builds up an unforgettable fictional portrait of two men and their commitment to their faith.

⮒ Read on
Shadows on the Rock
Brian Moore, *Black Robe* (a very different and bloodier tale of Catholic missionaries in the New World, set two centuries before Cather's novel); Thornton Wilder, *The Bridge of San Luis Rey*

TRACY CHEVALIER (b. 1962) USA/UK

GIRL WITH A PEARL EARRING (1999)
Born in America but a long-time resident of Britain, Tracy Chevalier came to prominence when *Girl with a Pearl Earring*, her historical novel set in seventeenth-century Holland, was published in 1999. It became a bestseller and the basis for an Oscar-nominated movie. The

novel cleverly takes a famous painting by Johannes Vermeer, the Delft artist who specialised in scenes of everyday life, and provides a story to explain the enigmatic woman who appears in it. In Chevalier's version of events, Griet is a naïve sixteen-year-old when she arrives in the painter's household as a maid. She is slowly drawn, despite the difference in age and social class, into an increasingly intimate relationship with her master, eventually acting as his muse and his model. Vermeer awakens something in Griet – 'he saw things in a way that others did not, so that a city I had lived in all my life seemed a different place', she says at one point in the novel – but the young woman also has a profound effect on the middle-aged painter. Through the eyes of Griet herself, we witness her perspective on the world, and his, slowly changing. Since the publication of *Girl with a Pearl Earring*, Tracy Chevalier has published three further novels, all of them set in the past. *Falling Angels* takes place in the years immediately after the death of Queen Victoria and looks at two families struggling to deal with the demands of the new century; *The Lady and the Unicorn* takes another work of art – a well-known series of fifteenth-century tapestries – and hangs a story of star-crossed lovers on the hook it provides; *Burning Bright* is a narrative which follows two children in late eighteenth-century London whose lives become entangled with that of the radical poet and artist William Blake. All three books have been successful but none has had quite the impact of the novel in which she brilliantly used a famous painting as a window into a past world.

◄ **Film versions:** *Girl with a Pearl Earring* (2003, with Scarlett Johansson as Griet and Colin Firth as Vermeer)

Read on

Falling Angels; *The Lady and the Unicorn*
Will Davenport, *The Painter* (a fictional episode in the life of Rembrandt); Deborah Moggach, *Tulip Fever*; Susan Vreeland, *Girl in Hyacinth Blue*

JAMES CLAVELL (1924–94) UK/USA

SHOGUN (1975)

Loosely based on the real-life adventures of William Adams, the first Englishman to live in Japan, Clavell's epic story is set in the year 1600. John Blackthorne, the character modelled on Adams, is acting as the pilot of a Dutch ship when it is shipwrecked on the Japanese coast. He and the other survivors of the wreck are taken captive by the local samurai. Thrust into an alien world, where the people and the customs are difficult to interpret, Blackthorne must learn to adapt and find ways to flourish. After saving the life of a powerful warlord named Toranaga, he enters his service and gradually wins the respect of the Japanese. Torn between the desire to return to his own country and his growing status and accomplishments in Japan, Blackthorne must decide where his future lies. James Clavell was the son of a British naval officer and he was serving in the armed forces himself when he was captured by the Japanese during the Second World War. He spent time in the notorious Changi prison in Singapore and his terrible experiences at this time were reflected in his first novel, *King Rat*, which was published in 1962. He became a bestselling author with this first book and went on to enjoy much further success both as a novelist and as a screenwriter. Chronologically, *Shogun* was the first in a loosely connected series of large-scale books Clavell wrote to which the collective title 'The Asian Saga' has sometimes been applied. The other books in the series range from *Tai-Pan*, a narrative set in nineteenth-century Hong Kong, to *Nobel House*, a story of political and financial hijinks in 1960s Hong Kong. All roared their way up the bestseller charts but none has quite the vigour and vitality of his tale of John Blackthorne's triumphs over adversity.

◾ **Film versions:** *Shogun* (1980, TV mini-series with Richard Chamberlain as Blackthorne)

🥢 **Read on**
Gai-jin; *Tai-Pan*
Conn Iggulden, *Wolf of the Plains*; Gary Jennings, *The Journeyer* (a novel about Marco Polo); James Michener, *Hawaii*; Eiji Yoshikawa, *Taiko* (feudal Japan as seen by the greatest Japanese historical novelist of the twentieth century)

BERNARD CORNWELL (b. 1944) UK

SHARPE'S EAGLE (1981)

Although he has published other series of historical novels, including one set in the Hundred Years War and one focusing on Alfred the Great and his wars against the Vikings, Bernard Cornwell remains best known for the Richard Sharpe books. These are largely set in the Napoleonic Wars and trace the rise from the ranks of their eponymous hero. *Sharpe's Eagle* was the first of the series to be published but it is not the first chronologically. Other novels, published later, delve further back into Sharpe's career. *Sharpe's Eagle* is set in 1809 and finds Cornwell's hero in Spain just before the Battle of Talavera. He and his group of sharpshooting riflemen are attached to a regiment commanded by Sir Henry Simmerson, a recurring villain in the series. Simmerson and his cronies lead the regiment to disaster and the loss of the regimental colours in an unnecessary confrontation with French dragoons. Only the capture of a French imperial 'eagle' in return will restore the regiment's honour and Sharpe soon discovers that his own future career may well hinge on such an act of heroism. In the fighting at Talavera his bitter conflict with Simmerson and the other, snobbish officers who despise him for his low birth reaches a climax and his courage stands in sharp contrast to their backstabbing and cowardice. In the very first book in the series, Sharpe shows all the qualities, both good and bad, which make him one of the convincing and engaging characters in military historical fiction. Subsequent novels recount his military exploits from the siege of Seringapatam and the war against Tipu Sultan in 1799 (*Sharpe's Tiger*) to the final campaign against

Napoleon in 1815 (**Sharpe's Waterloo**) and beyond. All the Sharpe books possess the energy and readability which have made Bernard Cornwell such a popular writer.

◣ Film version: *Sharpe's Eagle* (1993, one of a series of TV films made from Cornwell's novels and starring Sean Bean as Sharpe)

⮑ Read on
Sharpe's Gold; *Sharpe's Company* (and the other books in the 'Sharpe' series'), *Harlequin* (the first in the 'Grail Quest' series set in fourteenth century England and France)
Allan Mallinson, *A Close Run Thing*; Julian Stockwin, *Kydd*

LINDSEY DAVIS (b. 1949) UK

THE SILVER PIGS (1989)
In the last twenty years, historical crime fiction has become increasingly popular. One of its most successful sub-genres has been the crime novel set in ancient Rome and one of the best practitioners of this sub-genre has been Lindsey Davis. Her engaging hero Marcus Didius Falco, a private investigator walking the mean streets of the city in the time of the Emperor Vespasian, has appeared in eighteen books so far and there are undoubtedly many more to come. Falco begins the series as

the archetypal tough-guy gumshoe transported to ancient Rome but he has developed into a much more complex and engaging character during subsequent adventures. In the first novel in the series, he departs Rome to investigate a scam in the furthest flung and most godforsaken corner of the empire – Britain. Far from civilisation, he narrowly avoids a sticky end and forms an unlikely partnership with Helena Justina, an aristocratic Roman lady with attitude. Together they learn what has been happening in the silver mines that constitute Britannia's major asset for the Romans and uncover the conspiracy that is diverting silver ingots or 'pigs' from the imperial coffers into private hands. Since his first appearance in *The Silver Pigs*, Falco has travelled far. Lindsey Davis's novels have taken him from the forbidding forests of Germany (*The Iron Hand of Mars*) to the tourist sites of Greece (*See Delphi and Die*) and from North Africa (*Two for the Lions*) to the Middle East (*Last Act in Palmyra*). He has returned twice to Britain (in *A Body in the Bathhouse* and *The Jupiter Myth*) and visited just about every corner of the Roman empire. He has spawned a number of imitators but has deservedly retained his position as the best of all private eyes from the ancient world.

☙ Read on

Shadows in Bronze; *Venus in Copper* (and the other books in the Falco series)
Rosemary Rowe, *The Germanicus Mosaic*; Marilyn Todd, *I, Claudia*

READONATHEME: ANCIENT ROMAN MURDERS

Ron Burns, *Roman Nights*
Paul Doherty, *Murder Imperial*
R.S. Downie, *Ruso and the Disappearing Dancing Girls*
Jane Finnis, *Get Out or Die*
Barbara Hambly, *The Quirinal Hill Affair*
Albert Noyer, *The Cybeline Conspiracy*
Ben Pastor, *The Water Thief*
Simon Scarrow, *Under the Eagle*
David Wishart, *White Murder*

CHARLES DICKENS (1812–70) UK

A TALE OF TWO CITIES (1859)

Much of Dickens's fiction turned away from the contemporary London he knew as an adult and looked back to the city he remembered from his childhood but only two of the novels he wrote can truly be called historical fiction. One is *Barnaby Rudge*, a tale of murder and family intrigue set against the backdrop of violence and mob rule in the Gordon Riots of 1780. The other is *A Tale of Two Cities*, set during the French Revolution and the years leading up to it. 'It was the best of times, it was the worst of times', as the novel's famous opening words declare and the action of the novel is designed to prove them true. The two cities of the title are, of course, Paris and London. The action of the novel, which plays out over nearly twenty years, focuses on Lucie Manette, a Frenchwoman who grew up in England, and the two men who love her, Charles Darnay and Sydney Carton. Darnay is a French aristocrat who hates the injustice of the society in which his family flourished; Carton is a boozy, cynical London lawyer who, conveniently for the purposes of the plot, bears a striking resemblance to Darnay. When the Revolution begins, Darnay is safe in England and married to Lucie but he returns to Paris in an attempt to rescue an old family retainer. He is immediately arrested and there seems nothing that Lucie can do to save him. The guillotine looks to beckon for him but Carton, inspired by his ennobling love for Lucie, arranges to make the ultimate sacrifice. As Carton says, in the other famous quote from the novel, 'It is a far, far better thing that I do, than I have ever done; it is a far, far better rest that I go to than I have ever known.'

⬛ Film version: *A Tale of Two Cities* (1935, with Ronald Colman as Sydney Carton); *A Tale of Two Cities* (1958, with Dirk Bogarde as Carton)

📖 Read on
Barnaby Rudge
Harrison Ainsworth, *Rookwood*; ▶▶ Alexandre Dumas, *The Count of Monte Cristo*

E.L. DOCTOROW (b. 1931) USA

RAGTIME (1975)

Born in New York City, E.L. Doctorow was educated at Kenyon College, Ohio and Columbia University and had already published a number of well-received volumes of fiction while working as a book editor in the 1960s when his fourth novel, *Ragtime*, became a major critical and commercial succes. The book, set in the years immediately before the First World War, is not a conventional narrative but a sequence of interlinked vignettes. A family of Doctorow's invention, unnamed except in generic terms as Father, Mother and Mother's Younger Brother, leads a life of upper middle-class ease in the town of New Rochelle. An immigrant and his young daughter, newly arrived in the country, experience the worst hardships of poverty and the violence of industrial disputes before the father chances upon the path to prosperity. Coalhouse Walker, a black pianist based on a character from a classic German novel, is propelled into violence by prejudice, injustice and his own refusal to compromise his principles. Meanwhile the beautiful Evelyn Nesbit finds herself at the heart of the most scandalous murder case of the era when her husband Harry Thaw shoots her former lover, the architect Stanford White, the escapologist Harry Houdini enthrals the nation with his daring stunts and J.P. Morgan and Henry Ford meet to discuss the destiny of mankind. Doctorow's fictional characters mix with one another and with the real-life individuals to create a rich and rewarding literary mosaic. Doctorow has continued to find inspiration in the past in his more recent books. *The Waterworks* (1994) is a story of corruption, child abuse and a mad search for immortality in 1870s New York. *The March*, published in 2005, chronicles General Sherman's march to the sea in the last days of the American Civil War. However, none of Doctorow's other books has quite the same verve and originality that *Ragtime* possesses on every one of its pages.

📖 **Film version:** *Ragtime* (1981, directed by Milos Forman)

📚 **Read on**
The Waterworks; *The March*
Kevin Baker, *Dreamland*; Glen David Gold, *Carter Beats the Devil*; Dennis Lehane, *The Given Day*; Marge Piercy, *Sex Wars: A Novel of Gilded Age New York*

SIR ARTHUR CONAN DOYLE (1859–1930) UK

THE WHITE COMPANY (1891)
One of Sir Arthur Conan Doyle's greatest interests was military history and, famously, he regarded his historical fiction as his best work. His Sherlock Holmes stories, by contrast, he often considered as little more than potboilers written first to bring in money and then, later in his career, to satisfy public demand. Readers then and now have not agreed with him about the superiority of his historical novels to the stories of the great detective but several of his works in the genre are very definitely worth reading. The Brigadier Gerard stories, about a vainglorious but likeable soldier in Napoleon's armies, remain great

fun. *Rodney Stone*, set in the Regency period, makes effective use of Doyle's knowledge of the period and, particularly, of bare-knuckle boxing. However, Doyle's most ambitious historical fiction is set in the Middle Ages. *The White Company* follows the fortunes of Alleyne Edricson, a young man who leaves the seclusion of the monastery where he has grown up to enter the secular world. In a village pub, he encounters Samkin Aylward, a boisterous veteran of the wars in France, and Hordle John, a giant of a man who has also just left the religious life behind him. The three of them join forces and attach themselves to a troop of soldiers, under the command of Sir Nigel Loring, which is returning to the south of France to fight. The novel chronicles the adventures of Alleyne, Sam and John as they take their places amid the armies of the Black Prince and witness the greatest names in chivalry facing up to one another in tournament and on the battlefield. Eventually, after a desperate battle in northern Spain in which Alleyne distinguishes himself and a series of further trials and tribulations, the warriors return as heroes to Hampshire. Doyle had read and researched widely on the Middle Ages and, in *The White Company*, he drew upon his research to create a boys' own adventure story that remains thoroughly engaging and enjoyable more than a century after its first publication.

⮺ Read on

The Complete Brigadier Gerard Stories; *Sir Nigel* (the adventures as a young man of Sir Nigel Loring, one of the main characters in *The White Company*); *Rodney Stone*
Howard Pyle, *Men of Iron*; ▸▸ Robert Louis Stevenson, *The Black Arrow*

ALEXANDRE DUMAS (1802–70) FRANCE

THE THREE MUSKETEERS (1844)

Alexandre Dumas *père* was an improbably productive writer. Between his debut as a dramatist in the 1820s and his death in 1870, hundreds and hundreds of plays, novels, histories, travel journals, even cookbooks, poured forth from Parisian publishers under his name. He worked with dozens of collaborators, creating a kind of Dumas fictional workshop in which new stories could be collectively constructed. Of all the books he produced, the most famous, with the possible exception of *The Count of Monte Cristo*, is *The Three Musketeers*, a tale of swordsmanship and derring-do set in seventeenth-century France. The central character is D'Artagnan, a fiery young Gascon, who goes to Paris in the hope of joining the King's Musketeers. Once in the capital, he makes friends with Athos, Porthos and Aramis, three swordsmen already in the musketeers, largely by offering to fight with them all on the same day, and the four become inseparable. Once D'Artagnan is accepted into the royal service, he and the other musketeers find themselves thrown into the intrigue surrounding Louis XIII, his queen, Anne of Austria, and his chief minister, Cardinal Richelieu. The queen is unhappy in her marriage to the king and is attracted to the handsome Englishman, the Duke of Buckingham. Through his love for his landlady Constance Bonacieux, who also happens to be dressmaker and confidante to the queen, D'Artagnan is drawn into a scheme to allow Anne and Buckingham to meet. The queen hands her beau a set of diamonds that was a gift from Louis and Buckingham heads back to England. However, the queen's enemy Richelieu learns of this and arranges for a court ball to take place at which the jewels must be worn. D'Artagnan and his friends are despatched to England, with the Cardinal's men in pursuit, to rescue the diamonds. They succeed but they have now aroused the enmity of the all-powerful Richelieu and his agents, including the beautiful and mysterious Milady, and they must spend the rest of Dumas's rousing and swashbuckling yarn fighting for their lives and for their honours.

Film versions: *The Three Musketeers* (1973, directed by Richard Lester, with Michael York as D'Artagnan and Oliver Reed, Richard Chamberlain and Frank Finlay as his musketeer pals); *The Three Musketeers* (1993)

Read on
Twenty Years After; The Vicomte of Bragelonne (usually divided in English into three volumes of which one is 'The Man in the Iron Mask') >> Victor Hugo, *Ninety-Three* (set in the French Revolution); >> Rafael Sabatini, *Bellarion the Fortunate*

DAPHNE DU MAURIER (1907–89) UK

JAMAICA INN (1936)

Daphne Du Maurier's best-known and best-loved book is *Rebecca*, the story of a young girl who marries an enigmatic widower and goes to be mistress of his country home, Manderley, only to find it haunted by the mystery of his first wife's death. One of the great strengths of the novel was the power with which it conjured up the landscape of Cornwall in which its story was set. *Rebecca* appeared in 1938. Two years before, Du Maurier had published a book which raided the history of the same county to tell a tale of murder, shipwrecks and smuggling. Legends of hard-hearted 'wreckers' luring unwary vessels on to the rocks around the British coast and then plundering them of their goods have existed for centuries and Du Maurier makes great use of them in *Jamaica Inn*. The central character in the book is Mary Yellan, a woman in her early twenties, who goes to live with her aunt and uncle at the remote inn which gives the book its title. Jamaica Inn is a strange and forbidding place. No guests stay there and, indeed, it seems rarely to open for business of any kind. Mary's Uncle Joss is a brutal drunkard and his niece soon learns that he is also involved with a gang of wreckers. She finds herself attracted to Joss's younger brother, Jess, but the person in whom she eventually chooses to confide is the strange-looking albino vicar of a neighbouring parish, Francis Davey. As the novel progresses, she realises that her decision to trust in this representative of the church is misguided and that she has placed herself in the power of the very man most likely to harm her. One of Du Maurier's finest novels, *Jamaica Inn* takes the legends of the Cornish wreckers and incorporates them in a compelling, page-turning gothic romance.

🖿 **Film version:** *Jamaica Inn* (1939, directed by Alfred Hitchcock and starring Maureen O'Hara as Mary Yellan)

📚 **Read on**
Frenchman's Creek
J. Meade Falkner, *Moonfleet*; Winston Graham, *Ross Poldark* (first of a series set in eighteenth-century Cornwall); Russell Thorndike, *Doctor Syn*

DOROTHY DUNNETT (1923–2001) UK

NICCOLO RISING (1986)

Dorothy Dunnett was a professional portrait painter, a writer of detective stories and a member of the great and good in the cultural life of Scotland for many decades. She is best known, however, as the author of two long and involving sequences of historical novels. 'The Lymond Chronicles' recount, in six volumes, the adventures of a Scottish nobleman, Francis Crawford of Lymond, at large in sixteenth-century Europe. The eight volumes of 'The House of Niccolo', loosely connected to 'The Lymond Chronicles', were published later and set earlier. They record events in the fifteenth century and chart the rise and rise of their central character, Nicholas de Fleury, from humble dyer's apprentice to wealthy and powerful merchant. 'From Venice to Cathay, from Seville to the Gold Coast of Africa, men anchored their ships and opened their ledgers and weighed one thing against another as if nothing would ever change.' The very first sentence of *Niccolo Rising*, the first volume in the series, describes the world of trade that its central character will inhabit and into which he will bring changes which other, less dynamic merchants fail to imagine. The book opens in Bruges where the eighteen-year-old Claes is introduced to readers. Claes, a good-natured prankster with an eye for a pretty girl, at first seems an unlikely candidate for the role of mercantile hero. Yet he is sharp-eyed, adept with figures and swift to seize any opportunity that presents itself. As Dunnett's complicated narrative, with its huge cast list of characters, unfolds, Claes begins his transformation from lowly apprentice to man of substance. Later books will see him involved in adventures from Scotland to Russia as his power and influence expand across Europe. Rich in the authentic detail of the past, the volumes that make up 'The House of Niccolo', with their engaging and ever-developing protagonist, are amongst the most absorbing historical fiction of recent years.

🕮 Read on

Spring of the Ram; *Race of Scorpions* (and five more titles in 'The House of Niccolo' series); *The Game of Kings* (the first book in 'The Lymond Chronicles')

>> Sharon Kay Penman, *Here Be Dragons* (first in a trilogy about the princes of medieval Wales)

UMBERTO ECO (b. 1932) ITALY

THE NAME OF THE ROSE (1980)

Before publishing his first novel in his late forties, Umberto Eco was already a well-known figure in the Italian intellectual and cultural world. He began his academic career as a medievalist with a particular interest in Thomas Aquinas but he moved into the emerging field of semiotics and became the first professor of the subject at one of Europe's oldest universities, Bologna. *The Name of the Rose* was an enormous success, selling millions of copies worldwide, and it launched Eco on a parallel career as a novelist. On one level, this first novel is a murder mystery. During a visit to an Italian monastery, a fourteenth-century monk, tellingly named William of Baskerville, uses methods of deduction which anticipate those of Sherlock Holmes to solve a series of murders. The book is narrated by Adso of Melk, Baskerville's then youthful companion, who, in his old age, writes down the story of what happened to them when they arrived at the remote abbey. Whilst they are there several monks meet with bizarre deaths. (One is found head-down in a vessel of pig's blood.) Brother William pits his wits against the killer and realises that the key to the whole mystery lies with the labyrinthine library at the heart of the abbey and with its custodian, the blind scholar Jorge of Burgos. Eventually, through the application of reason and logic, he comes close to the truth. However, there is much more going on in the book than in the average whodunit. Through the story of William of Baskerville and his investigation, Eco is able to explore differing ideas about the nature of truth and the best way for fallible human beings to approach it. His gripping and demanding tale of mystery also becomes a celebration of open-mindedness and intelligence, of tolerance and the capacity to laugh at the follies and foibles of mankind.

📽 **Film version:** *The Name of the Rose* (1986, with Sean Connery as William of Baskerville and Christian Slater as Adso of Melk)

📚 **Read on**
Baudolino
John Barth, *The Sot-Weed Factor*; Luther Blissett, *Q*

READ ON A THEME: THE MIDDLE AGES

>> Peter Ackroyd, *The Clerkenwell Tales*
Tariq Ali, *A Sultan in Palermo*
Peter Benson, *Odo's Hanging*
Elizabeth Chadwick, *The Greatest Knight*
Alfred Duggan, *Count Bohemond*
Michael Jecks, *The Last Templar*
Edward Marston, *The Wolves of Savernake*
Robert Nye, *Falstaff*
Edith Pargeter (Ellis Peters), *A Bloody Field by Shrewsbury*
Candace Robb, *The Apothecary Rose*
Reay Tannahill, *The World, the Flesh and the Devil*

ROBERT EDRIC (b. 1956) UK

THE BOOK OF THE HEATHEN (2000)

Robert Edric is not the best known novelist of his generation but he is, arguably, the one who has produced the most exciting and adventurous historical fiction. Certainly he has been one of the most wide-ranging in his subject matter. He has written incisive and intelligent novels set in (among other places and times) nineteenth-century Tasmania at the time of the genocide of the indigenous people (*Elysium*), the Arctic wastes in the heroic era of European exploration (*The Broken Lands*) and Germany in the immediate aftermath of the Second World War (*The Kingdom of Ashes*). However, perhaps his best and most powerful novel is *The Book of the Heathen*. The story is told by James Frasier, an ordinary, decent man facing circumstances for which nothing in his previous life has prepared him. Frasier is a mapmaker but, when he travels to a small British trading post in the Belgian Congo, he finds himself on physical and moral territory for which no maps can be made. At the beginning of the book, Frasier's much-admired friend Nicholas Frere is in prison, charged with the seemingly senseless murder of a native girl. Frere refuses to deny any of the charges against him and awaits his inevitable conviction. As Edric's novel winds menacingly towards the devastating revelation of what really happened, the cruelties of colonialism and the mysteries of human motivation are gradually revealed. *The Book of the Heathen* revisits territory explored by Joseph Conrad in *Heart of Darkness* and it is set in 1897, only two years before that devastating novella was serialised in *Blackwood's Magazine*. From the end of the twentieth century, Edric looks back a century and fashions a story that has much of the dark power of Conrad's narrative.

Read on

Gathering the Water; *The Kingdom of Ashes*

Louis de Bernières, *Birds Without Wings*; Sebastian Faulks, *Human Traces*; Brian Moore, *The Magician's Wife*

THOMAS EIDSON USA

ST AGNES' STAND (1994)

The story is set in New Mexico in the mid-nineteenth century. Out in the wilderness Nat Swanson comes across two wagons surrounded by hostile Apache Indians. Swanson is on the run from a posse of men who blame him for a fatal shooting and he has every reason to avoid adding to his troubles by helping the party in the wagons. But the sight of an old woman's face glimpsed amongst those besieged by the Apaches stirs his humanity. The woman is Sister St Agnes, one of a group of nuns and orphans who have been ambushed by the Indians. She has been praying to God for a saviour and she has little doubt that Swanson is a heaven-sent deliverer. Swanson doubts this but he does indeed come to the assistance of the besieged travellers and, over the next five days, enables them to hold out and, eventually, escape. And, when Swanson is obliged to face his own nemesis, in the shape of the men who have been pursuing him, the sister has her own means of saving the man who has saved her. As a writer, Thomas Eidson has worked almost exclusively in the Western genre and *St Agnes' Stand* is, in many ways, a very traditional Western, the kind of story that could, in an earlier time, have been made into a film starring John Wayne or Gary Cooper. However, Eidson has ambitions to push back the boundaries of the genre and use it to explore ideas of choice and morality in ways characteristic of more 'literary' fiction. Later novels, such as *The Last Ride* (in which a woman and her estranged father join forces to rescue her young daughter from as gang of desperadoes) and *All God's Children* (about an unlikely alliance between a Quaker widow and a black petty thief), reveal these ambitions clearly enough but they were first and most successfully articulated in the gripping narrative that is *St Agnes' Stand*.

🕮 Read on

The Last Ride; *All God's Children*; *Souls of Angels*
Jim Fergus, *The Last Apache Girl*; Elmore Leonard, *Hombre*; Jack Schaefer, *Shane*

GEORGE ELIOT (1819–80) UK

ROMOLA (1863)

Marian Evans, best known as George Eliot, is universally recognised as one of the greatest of nineteenth-century novelists. She began her literary career as a translator of works from German and as an essayist and critic. Her first fiction was *Scenes of Clerical Life*, three stories which appeared under her male pseudonym in *Blackwood's Magazine* in 1857. *Adam Bede* was published in 1859 to great acclaim and was followed by a number of other novels, including *The Mill on the Floss*, *Silas Marner* and *Middlemarch*, usually considered her finest work. *Romola* was published in 1863 and is set in Florence at the height of the Renaissance. Its eponymous heroine is a scholar's daughter who yearns to play a noble role in the life of her city. She is attracted to the moral teachings of the reforming priest Savanorola who is intent upon the regeneration of the city and the scourging of the corrupt. She is also attracted to the clever and charming Tito Melema, a young man who has arrived in Florence after a shipwreck. They marry but, as the novel progresses, Romola's disillusionment with her husband deepens. Ambitious and unscrupulous, Tito is quite prepared to betray his adopted father (whom he refuses to redeem from slavery) and to deceive his wife by marrying another woman secretly and fathering children on her. The book charts Romola's gradual awakening to the truths about Tito and her education through suffering.

Now very much considered one of its author's lesser works, *Romola* deserves to be read more frequently than it probably is. George Eliot's recreation of the turbulent society of Renaissance Florence, shaken by religious and moral upheaval, and the portrait of her passionate heroine are both impressive. The author herself said that *Romola* was 'written with my best blood, such as it is, and with the most ardent care for veracity of which my nature is capable'. It is difficult to disagree with her.

📖 Read on

Nathaniel Hawthorne, *The Scarlet Letter*

READ ON A THEME: THE RENAISSANCE

Anna Banti, *Artemisia*
Sarah Dunant, *The Birth of Venus*
Elizabeth Eyre, *Death of the Duchess*
Joanne Harris, *Holy Fools*
Jeanne Kalogridis, *Painting Mona Lisa*
M.R. Lovric, *The Floating Book*
David Madsen, *Memoirs of a Gnostic Dwarf*
Jacqueline Park, *The Secret Book of Grazia dei Rossi*
Salman Rushdie, *The Enchantress of Florence*
Irving Stone, *The Agony and the Ecstasy*
Susan Vreeland, *The Passion of Artemisia*

MICHEL FABER (b. 1960)
NETHERLANDS/AUSTRALIA/UK

THE CRIMSON PETAL AND THE WHITE (2002)

Michel Faber was born in the Netherlands but moved to Australia with his family when he was a small boy. He went to university there and worked there (as a nurse) until he decided to emigrate to Scotland in the mid-1990s. It was in Scotland that he began to publish his fiction and it was a Scottish publisher, Canongate, which brought out his magnum opus, on which he had been working for years. *The Crimson Petal and the White* is a long and involving novel set in the Victorian era. At the heart of its epic narrative is Sugar, a teenage prostitute possessed of a determination to rise above the imprisoning circumstances to which fate seems to have condemned her. 'My name is Sugar,' she tells readers, 'I am a fallen woman, but I assure you: I did not fall. I was pushed.' The man doing most of the pushing is William Rackham, heir to a wealthy perfumer and husband of a 'madwoman in the attic' who sets up Sugar as his mistress. Intelligent, well-read and an aspiring writer (most of the characters in the novel are), the young prostitute becomes companion to William in ways that his poor, deluded wife cannot be. Through the story of Sugar and William, Faber presents a richly detailed panorama of Victorian England. When it appeared, the publisher billed *The Crimson Petal and the White* as 'the first great nineteenth-century novel of the twenty-first century' and that remains a clever description of the book. Rather as ›› John Fowles did thirty years earlier in *The French Lieutenant's Woman*, Faber uses many of the themes and motifs of Victorian fiction but he gives them a distinctly modern, indeed post-modern, twist. The story of Sugar gives readers many of the satisfactions provided by the great novelists of the nineteenth century but it never wants us to forget that it is also the product of a contemporary sensibility.

🕮 Read on

The Apple (subtitled 'Crimson Petal Stories', this is a collection of short stories featuring many of the characters from the novel)

Michael Cox, *The Meaning of Night*; D.J. Taylor, *Kept: A Victorian Mystery*

READ ON A THEME: NINETEENTH CENTURY NARRATIVES

>> Beryl Bainbridge, *Watson's Apology*
Jim Crace, *Signals of Distress*
>> Robert Edric, *Gathering the Water*
Margaret Forster, *Lady's Maid*
Sheri Holman, *The Dress Lodger*
Claude Izner, *The Père-Lachaise Mystery*
Jem Poster, *Rifling Paradise*
Belinda Starling, *The Journal of Dora Damage*
Will Thomas, *Some Danger Involved*
James Wilson, *The Dark Clue*

J.G. FARRELL (1935–79) UK

THE SIEGE OF KRISHNAPUR (1973)

J.G. Farrell died in his forties when he was swept into the sea while fishing off the coast of Ireland but, by the time of his death, he was already recognised as one of the most interesting and engaging novelists of his generation. His best fiction draws its stories and themes from the history of the British Empire. *Troubles* takes place in Ireland at the end of the First World War; *The Singapore Grip* follows the fortunes of a wide range of individuals caught up in the Japanese invasion of

Malaya during the Second World War. *The Siege of Krishnapur*, winner of the Booker Prize in 1973, is set in India at the time of the so-called Mutiny. In the (fictional) town of Krishnapur the white inhabitants struggle at first to take seriously the rumours of restless natives and sepoy uprising. Only Hopkins, the Collector, realises that something is genuinely amiss and, by the time his intuitions prove correct, the British in Krishnapur are under siege. As the siege develops, they find it increasingly difficult to cling to the beliefs that shaped them. The Collector, an admirer of the Great Exhibition, is hard pressed to retain his convictions about the inevitability of progress. Others see their ideas of the inherent superiority of white over native crumble and their faith in the Empire falter. Rich in character and action, Farrell's tragi-comedy of imperial misrule and incomprehension is unlike any other novel of the Raj. 'For a novel to be witty is one thing,' one reviewer wrote at the time of the book's first publication, 'to tell a good story is another, to be serious is yet another, but to be all three is surely enough to make it a masterpiece.' More than thirty years later, *The Siege of Krishnapur* does, indeed, seem some kind of masterpiece.

≋ Read on

Troubles; *The Singapore Grip*
Philip Hensher, *The Mulberry Empire*; ›› Julian Rathbone, *The Mutiny*

PATRICIA FINNEY (b. 1958) UK

FIREDRAKE'S EYE (1992)

Under her own name and pseudonyms, Patricia Finney has been writing historical fiction, mostly set in Tudor England, since she was in her late teens. As P.F. Chisholm, she has produced a series of crime novels set in the north of England during the reign of Elizabeth I. The 'Lady Grace' mystery stories, aimed at the young adult market, are written as if extracted from the 'daybooke' of Grace Cavendish, a maid of honour at Elizabeth's court. Her finest novels, however, are the three books featuring the cryptographer Simon Ames, a converted Portuguese Jew employed by the spymaster-general Sir Francis Walsingham, and his colleague in espionage, David Becket. Of these the first is *Firedrake's Eye*, set in London in 1583. The Protestant Elizabeth I has been on the throne for a quarter of a century and has been the target of Catholic plots to assassinate her and restore the old faith to England for most of those years. Now yet another is in the making.

'It was I that saw most and have said least in the matter of the firedrake and the nightcrow, the soldier of God and the hunting of that fair white hind, the Queen of England.' So Ralph Strangways, a young man committed to the madhouse by his own brother and also known as 'Poor Tom' or 'Tom o'Bedlam', introduces himself in the opening chapter of the novel and he remains at the heart of the mystery that Ames and Becket must unravel. As they venture into the dangerous underworld of Tudor London in search of the truth, Finney comes into her own as a writer. Her vivid use of language and her gift for lively characterisation give *Firedrake's Eye* and the two connected but self-contained books that followed it (*Unicorn's Blood*; *Gloriana's Torch*) an energy that sets them above most other historical crime novels.

🕮 Read on
Unicorn's Blood; *Gloriana's Torch*
P.F. Chisholm, *A Famine of Horses*; Michael Clynes, *The White Rose Murders*; Elizabeth Redfern, *Auriel Rising*; Leonard Tourney, *The Player's Boy Is Dead*

PENELOPE FITZGERALD (1916–2000) UK

THE BLUE FLOWER (1995)
Penelope Fitzgerald did not begin to publish fiction until she was in her sixties and her earlier novels, such as *The Bookshop* and the Booker Prize-winning *Offshore*, drew on her own experiences to create ironic and idiosyncratic novels of everyday life. She turned to historical fiction with books such as *The Beginning of Spring*, set in Moscow just before the upheavals of the First World War and the Russian Revolution, and *The Gate of Angels*, the story of a naïve academic in Edwardian Cambridge and his awkward attempts to win the love of a young woman. *The Blue Flower* was Fitzgerald's last novel and focuses on the German Romantic poet Friedrich von Hardenberg, or 'Fritz' as the novel most usually refers to him, better known by his pseudonym Novalis. The

title of the book comes from an unfinished and posthumously published work by Novalis in which the hero dreams of a blue flower and it becomes the focus of all his love and longing. (The 'blue flower' was adopted as a symbol of romantic yearning by later German writers.) The focus of Fitzgerald's story is Fritz's love for an ordinary young girl, Sophie von Kuhn. This love is questioned by friends who fail to see the attraction of an unremarkable and slightly dim young girl. It is fated to remain unconsummated and unfulfilled (Sophie dies of TB when she is barely into her teens) but it gives Fritz's life the meaning it lacked. Penelope Fitzgerald tells her story with brilliant economy. Her language is precise and unpretentious and she has the gift of summoning up the past through the description of what seem, at first, insignificant details of dress and speech and manner. *The Blue Flower* tells a tragic story of lost love with great wit and charm, and provides one of the most convincing of all fictional portraits of genius at large in the everyday world.

🕮 Read on

The Gate of Angels
>> Beryl Bainbridge, *According to Queeney*; >> Hilary Mantel, *Fludd*

KEN FOLLETT (b. 1949) UK

THE PILLARS OF THE EARTH (1989)

Ken Follett has been one of the bestselling British writers of the last thirty years and Second World War thrillers like *The Eye of the Needle* (his first major triumph) have been particularly successful. Yet the book that is nearest to his heart (and, to judge by sales, nearest to the hearts of his readers) is *The Pillars of the Earth*, set some eight centuries before the Second World War. Follett is a gripping storyteller and, in the building of a cathedral in the fictional medieval city of Kingsbridge, he found his ideal subject. The minute details of everyday life, all meticulously researched, combine with the large-scale drama of the slow rising of the great monument to God to create a novel that embodies both the beauty and the cruelty of the age in which it is set. Follett constructs a vast canvas on which to work but his greatest triumphs are his characters. The entwining stories of Tom the master mason, Lady Aliena, the prior Philip and dozens of others are vividly brought to life and their loves, fears and obsessions provide the driving force for the vast, sprawling narrative. Follett returned to medieval Kingsbridge in *World Without End*, published in 2007, although it is the town as it is two hundred years later than the events chronicled in *The Pillars of the Earth*. The characters are descendants of the men and women who peopled the earlier novel. At the opening of the book, the year is 1327 and four children from the cathedral city are witnesses to a double killing in the forest surrounding it. The repercussions of the unexplained murders continue to haunt all of them as their very different destinies unfold. Taken together, *The Pillars of the Earth* and *World*

Without End form an epic narrative of medieval England which is Follett's finest achievement.

🐃 Read on

World Without End

Marilyn Durham, *Flambard's Confession*; Ildefonso Falcones, *Cathedral of the Sea*; ›› William Golding, *The Spire* (a very different writer tells a story of the building of a medieval cathedral); Edward Rutherfurd, *London*

FORD MADOX FORD (1873–1939) UK

THE FIFTH QUEEN (1906–8)

The son of the German-born music critic of *The Times* and originally called Ford Hermann Hueffer, Ford Madox Ford was one of the great figures of English literary modernism. After publishing many books under the name of Ford Madox Hueffer, he settled on the final version of his name at the end of the First World War, when anti-German feelings still ran high. By that time, he had already gained a reputation as an editor, essayist and writer of fiction. He had published two novels in collaboration with Joseph Conrad and *The Good Soldier*, the book that is often considered his finest achievement, had appeared in 1915. He had also published the three books (*The Fifth Queen*, *Privy Seal* and *The Fifth Queen Crowned*) which together form the trilogy usually known by just the title of the first volume. The queen in the title is Katharine Howard. Katharine, clever, beautiful and courageous, catches the eye of the ageing Henry VIII and becomes his fifth wife. The Tudor court, riven by faction and struggles for power, is a dangerous and claustrophobic place. The question of religion divides both palace and people and Katharine, a devotee of older forms of Catholicism, finds herself pitted against a formidable opponent in the Lord Privy Seal, Thomas Cromwell, who is at the forefront of religious reform. Tragedy lurks in the wings, waiting to arrive on stage. Ford, whose English grandfather was the Pre-Raphaelite painter Ford Madox Brown, wrote a number of books on art, including a study of Hans Holbein, Henry's court painter. Ford's portraits of the Tudor great and good may not always be historically accurate (there is little evidence that the real Katharine was much like his fictional version of her) but they have the solidity and conviction that the painter gave to his.

☙ Read on
Ladies Whose Bright Eyes (a curious time-travelling tale of a modern man going back to the medieval era, inspired by Ford's reading of Mark Twain's *A Connecticut Yankee at the Court of King Arthur*)
Bryher, *The Player's Boy*

C.S. FORESTER (1899–1966) UK

THE HAPPY RETURN (1937)

Born in Cairo, where his father was a civil servant in the Egyptian government, Forester studied medicine before turning to writing the fiction for which he is remembered. His work includes crime fiction, a comedy thriller, *The African Queen* (about a prissy missionary and a rough-diamond ship's captain who take a leaky old boat full of dynamite down an African river in the First World War to blow up an enemy convoy and fall in love on the way) which is better known in its film version starring Humphrey Bogart and Katharine Hepburn, and biographies of historical figures. However, by far his best known books are the volumes in the Hornblower series which trace the career, from midshipman to admiral, of Horatio Hornblower, a naval hero of the Napoleonic Wars. The first of these to be published (although not the first in chronological order of Hornblower's career) was *The Happy Return*. The year is 1808 and Hornblower is captain of HMS *Lydia*. He and his ship have been despatched by the Admiralty to Central America to make contact with revolutionaries who are about to take arms against the Spanish rulers of Nicaragua. Since Spain is allied with Napoleon and counts as one of England's enemies, Hornblower is instructed to assist the leader of the revolutionaries, Don Julian Alvarado, but he discovers him to be near to madness, a megalomaniac who insists on the soubriquet of El Supremo and is as much danger to his allies as his enemies. Trouble clearly lies ahead for Hornblower and his difficulties are only worsened by the distracting presence of Lady Barbara Wellesley, destined to become his second wife in a later book.

Forester went on to develop Hornblower over more than a dozen books and nearly thirty years, and to write extensively about his career before 1808, but *The Happy Return* remains the best place to be introduced to one of the greatest of all characters in naval fiction.

📖 Read on
A Ship of the Line; *Flying Colours*; *Lieutenant Hornblower* (and the other books in the 'Hornblower' series)
C. Northcote Parkinson, ***Devil to Pay***; Dudley Pope, ***Ramage***

JOHN FOWLES (1926–2005) UK

THE FRENCH LIEUTENANT'S WOMAN (1969)
The fiction of John Fowles first came to readers' attentions in the 1960s and *The French Lieutenant's Woman* gained much critical and commercial success when it was published. In one sense, it is a straightforward story, set in the nineteenth century, about the obsessive love between a rich man and the 'French Lieutenant's woman' of its title. Charles Smithson and Sarah Woodruff, a woman already stigmatised by her seduction and abandonment by a French naval officer, meet in the seaside town of Lyme Regis. They embark on an affair which scandalises society. She runs away; he pursues her. Fowles's prose, likewise, is for much of the time straightforward and

solid in the nineteenth-century manner. But he also plays games with the reader. He keeps interrupting the story to tell us things about Lyme Regis (home of Mary Anning the fossil collector), Darwin, Freudian psychology and the social customs of Victorian London. He claims that he has no idea what will happen next, that this is the characters' story, not his. He supplies alternative endings, so that we can choose between them. *The French Lieutenant's Woman* becomes a story which could only have been written in our own era. In the thirty-six years between the appearance of *The French Lieutenant's Woman* and his death, Fowles published only three works of fiction. Of these, only *A Maggot* qualifies as historical fiction. Set in the eighteenth century, it reworks a real-life murder investigation to take in erotic obsession, witchcraft, religious mania and flying saucers. It is as strange and unsettling a story as that of Charles Smithson and Sarah Woodruff. Fowles was one of the great innovators in modern English fiction. When he ventured into the past for his narratives, it is perhaps no great surprise that he came up with two books that play games with the very idea of what the historical novel can be.

📖 **Film version:** *The French Lieutenant's Woman* (1981, scripted by Harold Pinter and starring Jeremy Irons as Smithson and Meryl Streep as Sarah Woodruff)

📚 **Read on**
A Maggot
Jean Rhys, *Wide Sargasso Sea*; Graham Swift, *Waterland*

GEORGE MACDONALD FRASER (1925–2008)
UK

FLASHMAN (1969)

In the late 1960s, George MacDonald Fraser had the brilliant idea of taking the character of Flashman, school bully in Thomas Hughes's 1857 novel *Tom Brown's Schooldays*, and providing him with a future career. This career is described in what purport to be Flashman's memoirs, written as an old man basking in the glory of his reputation as a Victorian hero. In these memoirs, Flashman is shamelessly honest in revealing that this reputation is based on nothing more than outrageous luck. The very first volume (*Flashman*) begins with his expulsion from Rugby and sees him embarking on a military career in Lord Cardigan's Hussars. In Afghanistan, where he is despatched, the worst disaster in imperial history unfolds and thousands of British soldiers are slaughtered on the retreat from Kabul but Flashman is the one person to emerge from it smelling of roses. Discovered, unconscious and draped in the Union Jack, the only survivor of an Afghan assault on Piper's Fort (he was actually trying to hide), he returns to England a hero. In further volumes of the Flashman Papers, published over the next thirty years, Macdonald's anti-hero continues to lead an eventful life. He is stranded on the island of Madagascar where he becomes the toyboy of a depraved and lunatic native queen (*Flashman's Lady*). He is made a special ambassador to the court of a nymphomaniac maharani where he finds himself temporary guardian of the legendary Koh-i-Noor diamond (*Flashman and the Mountain of Light*). He rides into the American West and is ducking and dodging for cover as Custer's Seventh Cavalry and Sitting Bull's Sioux braves battle it out at the Little Big Horn (*Flashman and the Redskins*). Throughout his various adventures he is consistent only in his devotion to saving his own skin (at the expense of others, if necessary) and his urge to bed every attractive woman he meets. The Flashman books are wonderfully rude, funny, inventive and the most enjoyable means so far devised of learning about the empire in its Victorian heyday.

➽ Read on

Royal Flash; *Flash for Freedom!*; *Flashman at the Charge* (and the further eight books in the Flashman series)
Boris Akunin, *The Winter Queen*; John Biggins, *A Sailor of Austria*; ≫
Julian Rathbone, *A Very English Agent*

CHARLES FRAZIER (b. 1950) USA

COLD MOUNTAIN (1997)

At the heart of Charles Frazier's remarkable debut novel is W.P. Inman, a Confederate soldier in the American Civil War who is weary of the fighting. As the novel opens, he is recovering from a near-fatal wound and he has spent the long weeks in his hospital bed 'picturing the old green places he recollected from home'. Eventually he decides to desert. He sets off through the war-torn landscape of North Carolina on a long, long walk home to Cold Mountain where, he hopes and believes, his beloved Ada will still be waiting for him. In the meanwhile Ada is herself struggling to maintain the farmstead she has inherited after the death of her father. Throughout her upbringing, she has been sheltered from life's harsher realities and the battle to wrest a living from the land is one she is losing before the arrival of Ruby, a tough and resourceful young woman, who throws in her lot with Ada. Together, they work to bring the farm back to life. As Inman plods grimly on, facing the dangers of hunger and robbery and murderous Confederate guards forever on the look out for deserters, the two women continue to face their own tribulations. When the rendezvous for which Inman has yearned finally takes place, fate has one further twist to inflict on them all. After *Cold Mountain* became a huge bestseller, Frazier worked for nine years on a second novel, *Thirteen Moons*, another work of historical fiction set both in the Civil War and further back in America's past. Its tale of an ancient frontiersman recalling nine decades of his life could not match the success, both critical and commercial, of Frazier's first book. An odyssey that embodies the persistence of love and the endurance of hope, *Cold Mountain* is one of the most moving American novels of recent decades.

◣ **Film version:** *Cold Mountain* (2003, directed by Anthony Minghella and starring Jude Law as Inman and Nicole Kidman as Ada)

🥢 **Read on**
Thirteen Moons
Howard Bahr, *The Black Flower*; Louis de Bernières, *Captain Corelli's Mandolin* (another story of love threatened by war); David Fuller, *Sweetsmoke*

MARGARET GEORGE (b. 1943) USA

THE MEMOIRS OF CLEOPATRA (1997)

Margaret George is an American novelist, born in Nashville, Tennessee, who has made her name writing massive, thoroughly researched narratives in which historical figures supposedly tell their own stories. The first of these, *The Autobiography of Henry VIII*, appeared in the 1980s and proved a great success. It takes a high degree of chutzpah to provide an autobiographical voice for a historical figure as well known as Henry but Margaret George carried off her fictional impersonation with great conviction and her interpolations in the voice of the king's jest, Will Somers, only added to the reader's enjoyment. *The Memoirs of Cleopatra*, her third novel, is, like her first, exactly what its title suggests – the life of Cleopatra as narrated by the Egyptian queen herself. Beginning with her hazy recollections of the drowning of her mother when Cleopatra was three years old, the novel carries readers through the familiar dalliances with powerful Romans to the tragic denouement of her story when she plots her own death rather than submit to the humiliations planned by her enemies. Neatly combining the fruits of historical research with many incidents that had their origins in her own fertile imagination, Margaret George produced another huge and engrossing historical blockbuster. Since the publication of her Cleopatra novel, Margaret George has clearly decided that her forte is fiction in which the central character is a woman poised somewhere between history and legend. *Mary, Called Magdalene* makes much use of research into the era when Jesus and his disciples lived but, in the absence of any real historical data about her subject, Margaret George allows her imagination full rein to create a credible portrait of the woman who is one of the most mysterious characters in the Bible. *Helen of Troy* similarly tells a story set in that nebulous but productive territory where historical fact and mythological fancy meet. It is one that Margaret George has recently made her own.

≋ Read on
The Autobiography of Henry VIII; *Helen of Troy*
Amanda Elyot, *The Memoirs of Helen of Troy*; Colin Falconer, *When We Were Gods* (a different, male take on the story of Cleopatra); ›› Colleen McCullough, *Antony and Cleopatra*; Michelle Moran, *Nefertiti*

WILLIAM GOLDING (1911–93) UK

RITES OF PASSAGE (1980)
Lord of the Flies, William Golding's first novel, remains his most familiar. Its story of a group of schoolboys reverting to savagery after they are marooned on a desert island is a typical expression of its author's gloomy view of human nature. In Golding's world, viciousness and evil forever lurk beneath the surface of reason and virtue. Nearly thirty years later when he came to write *Rites of Passage*, the first book in a trilogy usually given the collective title of *To the Ends of the Earth*, his awareness of man's potential for cruelty remained acute. The trilogy follows the slow progress of a ship sailing to Australia in the early years

of the nineteenth century. The narrator of *Rites of Passage* (and the later volumes) is a young aristocrat named Edmund Talbot who is writing a journal of his experiences on board ship. Talbot is, in many ways, an unlikely and unlikeable hero. He is a snob, both socially and intellectually, overweeningly proud of his classical education and his connections to aristocracy. On his way to New South Wales to take up a post in the government there, obtained for him through the influence of his godfather, he is determined that his place in the social hierarchy should be acknowledged and respected. As the ship sails ever south-wards, the elements of tragedy are beginning to fall into place. Also on board is a priggish and insecure parson, from a lowly background, named Colley. At first, Colley's inability to mix with his fellow passengers and with the crew seems nothing more than a minor irritant on the voyage but, when the ship 'crosses the line', he faces a humiliation that ultimately destroys him. *Rites of Passage* works superbly as a self-enclosed story in itself but it also provides the opening for the longer tale of Talbot's journey towards greater maturity and self-awareness which Golding went on to complete in the two further volumes of his trilogy.

📽 **Film version:** *To the Ends of the Earth* (2005, TV miniseries based on the whole trilogy)

🥢 **Read on**
Close Quarters; *Fire Down Below* (the other books in the trilogy)
Richard Hughes, *A High Wind in Jamaica*

ROBERT GRAVES (1895–1985) UK

I, CLAUDIUS (1934)

Robert Graves believed himself to be, first and foremost, a poet. His novels, he always claimed, were mere potboilers written for the money he needed to buy himself the time to write his poetry. Those who have read his fiction might well disagree with him. The best of it is very good indeed and most of the best of it is set in the past. *Count Belisarius* takes place in sixth-century Byzantium; two novels featuring the heroic Sergeant Lamb are set in the American War of Independence; *Wife to Mr Milton* looks at the marital misalliance of the seventeenth century poet and his first wife; *They Hanged My Saintly Billy* is a fascinating take on the true story of the Victorian poisoner William Palmer. However, much the most rewarding of Graves's novels is *I, Claudius*. This book and its sequel, *Claudius the God*, are written as if they were autobiographical works by the fourth Roman emperor. 'I, Tiberius Claudius Drusus Nero Germanicus, this-that-and-the-other (for I shall not trouble you yet with all my titles),' the novel begins, 'who was once, and not so long ago either, known to my friends and relatives and associates as "Claudius the Idiot", or "That Claudius", or "Claudius the Stammerer", or "Clau-Clau-Claudius" or at best as "Poor Uncle Claudius", am now about to write this strange history of my life.' The opening sentence immediately establishes the memorable voice in which Graves tells his story. Disabled and epileptic, Claudius is an unlikely candidate for the Imperial throne but, regarded by others as a harmless fool, he survives the murderous dynastic intrigues of the early Roman Empire and the dangerous reigns of three predecessors to be presented with the highest office in a palace coup. With their cast of extraordinary characters, from Augustus, the founder of the dynasty, and his wife Livia to the megalomaniac Caligula, and the sheer energy of their narratives, Graves's two Claudius books remain some of the most readable fiction about the Roman Empire ever written.

🍖 **Film version:** *I, Claudius* (1976, TV series with Derek Jacobi as Claudius)

🕮 **Read on**
Claudius the God; *Count Belisarius*; *Wife to Mr Milton*
Allan Massie, *Augustus* (the first in a sequence about the early emperors of Rome) ▶▶ Gore Vidal, *Julian* (the story of the pagan Roman emperor Julian the Apostate as told largely in his own words)

PHILIPPA GREGORY (b. 1954) UK

THE QUEEN'S FOOL (2004)

Mary Tudor gets a poor press from many historians and novelists. Bloody Mary, presiding over a Catholic government that burned Protestant martyrs at the stake, is one of England's least popular monarchs. In Philippa Gregory's novel she is a more sympathetic figure. Driven by duty, even when deserted by those she loves, she is more of a tragic heroine – certainly a more likeable character than her sister, Elizabeth, a flirtatious coquette intent only on her own selfish ends. The true heroine of the novel, however, is Philippa Gregory's creation, Hannah Verde, the queen's fool of the title. Hannah is a hidden Jew, on the run from the Inquisition, who, thanks to her unpredictable ability to foresee the future, becomes the servant and confidante of both women. Caught between conflicting loyalties and mesmerised by the glamour of the handsome schemer Robert Dudley, Hannah struggles to survive in the dangerous world she inhabits. *The Queen's Fool* is one of a very loosely connected sequence of novels set in the Tudor period which Philippa Gregory has written. Thanks to the film version, the best known of these is *The Other Boleyn Girl,* in which the claustrophobic court of Henry VIII is seen through the eyes of Mary Boleyn, sister of the more famous Anne. Gregory has also written fiction set in other historical places and periods, from eighteenth century Bristol at the height of its slave trade prosperity (*A Respectable Trade*) to the American colonies in the early years of their settlement (*Virgin Earth*). However, there is no doubt that the years of the Tudor monarchs provide her with the canvas for her finest fiction and *The Queen's Fool*, with its brilliant portrait of an outsider at the heart of Mary's court, has some claims to being the best of all her books.

🕮 Read on
The Other Boleyn Girl, The Other Queen (Mary, Queen of Scots)
Karen Essex, *Leonardo's Swans*; Alison Weir, *Innocent Traitor* (Lady Jane Grey)

KATE GRENVILLE (b. 1950) AUSTRALIA

THE SECRET RIVER (2005)

Kate Grenville's imaginative reconstruction of the early years of white Australia focuses on William and Sal Thornhill, transported from London to New South Wales in 1807. At first they dream of the day they will return to the banks of the Thames but eventually they are obliged to recognise that the dream will not become reality and that they must create a new life for themselves in an alien land. Opportunity for betterment presents itself in the shape of supposedly unclaimed land up the Hawkesbury River and away from the primitive settlements of Sydney. Will is eager to establish himself as a man of property but, when he and Sal and their expanding family turn their backs on the township and move up-river, they find the land is not quite as empty as they believed. Aboriginal people are already there. As two utterly different cultures, each incapable of understanding the other, come face to face, the stage is set for tragedy. Will, a fundamentally decent man, struggles to reconcile his desire to possess a piece of land which can be 'the blank page on which a man might write a new life' and his desire to live in peace with neighbours both white and black. In the end he finds it impossible to do so and is forced into a decision which involves him in an act of terrible violence that haunts him for the rest of his life. Kate Grenville is one of the subtlest Australian novelists of her generation. *The Idea of Perfection*, her 1999 novel about two unlikely lovers in a small New South Wales town, won the Orange Prize for Fiction. Deservedly shortlisted for the Booker Prize in the year it was published, *The Secret River* is a poignant exploration of the human losses and gains involved in the creation of white Australia.

🐚 Read on

Dark Places; *The Lieutenant* (the story of a soldier who arrived in Australia on the First Fleet and his poignant relationship with an Aboriginal child)

Carol Birch, *Scapegallows*; **»** Colleen McCullough, *Morgan's Run*

READ ON A THEME: AUSTRALIA FAIR AND FOUL

Bryce Courtenay, *The Potato Factory*
Eleanor Dark, *The Timeless Land*
Richard Flanagan, *Gould's Book of Fish*
» Thomas Keneally, *Bring Larks and Heroes*
Joan Lindsay, *Picnic at Hanging Rock*
David Malouf, *The Conversations at Curlow Creek*
Roger McDonald, *The Ballad of Desmond Kale*

ROBERT HARRIS (b. 1957) UK

POMPEII (2003)

Originally a political journalist, Robert Harris became a bestselling novelist with his first work of fiction, *Fatherland*, set in an alternative reality where the Nazis have won the Second World War and, in the Berlin of 1964, preparations are under way for the celebration of Hitler's seventy-fifth birthday. Other equally successful novels followed, each one taking some aspect of twentieth-century history (code-breaking in World War Two, the opening up of Soviet archives in the age of glasnost) and making it the basis of gripping fiction. It came as something of a surprise when Harris turned his attention to more distant historical events but *Pompeii*, a thriller set in first-century Italy at the time of the devastating eruption of Vesuvius, proved that he could use ancient history to underpin his narratives just as skilfully as he could elaborate on the recent past. The novel's central character is Marcus Attilius Primus, a young hydraulic engineer who has been put in charge of the aqueduct that provides the towns around the Bay of Naples with their water. Mysteries surround Attilius from the moment he takes up his position. His predecessor has vanished and there are problems with the aqueduct and the water supply. With the backing of Pliny, a famous scholar who is also the admiral in charge of Roman naval forces in the region, Attilius sets off across the bay and climbs Mount Vesuvius to discover what is happening. He comes across evidence of human corruption and villainy but soon everything is overshadowed by the inhuman violence of nature. The eruption of the volcano renders the petty concerns of the ordinary world meaningless and Attilius is thrust into a nightmare of death and destruction. Against the backdrop of implacable natural forces, he is obliged to engage in an apparently impossible fight for survival. *Pompeii* proved that Harris could bring the distant past to life as vividly as recent history or an alternative future.

🐦 Read on
Enigma (set in Bletchley Park, the code-breaking centre during the Second World War); *Imperium* (the second of Harris's Roman novels)
Edward Bulwer Lytton, *The Last Days of Pompeii* (for a very different, nineteenth-century version of the same events)

GEORGETTE HEYER (1902–74) UK

A CIVIL CONTRACT (1961)
Georgette Heyer began publishing romances in the 1920s and, more than thirty years after her death, many are still in print. She is most famous for stories set in the Regency period (*Regency Buck*, published in 1935, was the first of these) but she also wrote fiction that took place in a variety of historical settings from Norman Europe (*The Conqueror*) to England under the rule of Oliver Cromwell (*Royal Escape*). Heyer is often dismissed as the author of fluffy love stories about brooding heroes and swooning heroines but, as her continuing popularity suggests, she was much more than that. Her books continue to attract readers because they are rich in convincing period detail, well-written and gloriously entertaining. And many of her later novels have a depth

to them that would surprise readers who know the author only by reputation. One of the best of these is *A Civil Contract*. It hero is Adam Deveril, newly become Viscount Lynton, who returns from heroic endeavours in the Peninsular War to discover that the family estate is teetering on the brink of bankruptcy and his inheritance looks likely to disappear beneath a sea of debts. The only option seems to be to turn his back on his first love, the glamorous Julia Oversley, and enter on a marriage of convenience with Jenny Chawleigh, the dowdy daughter of a man distinguished only by his wealth. The story of what happens after the marriage is not by any means the conventional romance with which Heyer's name is so closely associated but it has a tenderness and a truth to life that readers may well find even more appealing. At the end of *A Civil Contract* it is the ordinary and the everyday that turns out to be 'really much more important than grand passions or blighted loves'.

🕮 Read on
The Grand Sophy; *An Infamous Army*; *Regency Buck*; *Sprig Muslin*
Jean Plaidy, *The Captive of Kensington* (the young Queen Victoria as romantic heroine); Amanda Quick, *With This Ring* (first in a series of contemporary 'Regency romances')

PETER HO DAVIES (b. 1966) UK

THE WELSH GIRL (2007)

Peter Ho Davies, the son of Welsh and Chinese parents, had published two critically acclaimed volumes of short stories and had already been chosen as one of the 2003 'Granta Best of Young British Novelists' before he even published his first novel. When it finally appeared, *The Welsh Girl*, a story set during the Second World War, justified all the high expectations many people had of it. It is a remarkable work of historical fiction, one that revels in the ordinariness of its characters and focuses not so much on the people remembered in history books as on the unexceptional lives of those we are only too likely to forget. The year is 1944 and Esther, the Welsh girl of the title, is seventeen years old, the daughter of a fiercely nationalistic hill farmer, contemptuous of the English soldiers drafted into the midst of his isolated community. Esther herself, dreaming of an escape to the wider world she glimpses in infrequent trips to the cinema, is less certain that she despises the English incomers. She even enters a brief relationship with one of them, only for it to end in a brutal disillusionment. Meanwhile, a POW camp has been built in the hills near the village and the first inmates, German soldiers captured during the Normandy landings, begin to arrive. Karsten is a young NCO, barely out of his teens, who is haunted by the thought that the surrender which has saved his life has made him less of a man than those who fought on. To the Welsh villagers, the POWs are the dehumanised representatives of an otherwise distant enemy. Yet, when Karsten escapes from the camp, Esther finds that the simple categorisations of friend and foe she has adopted are difficult to maintain. Poignant and perceptive, *The Welsh Girl* explores the ways in which individuals define their own identities and loyalties to place and people in times of war.

☙ Read on

Sadie Jones, *The Outcast*; Owen Sheers, *Resistance*

VICTOR HUGO (1802–85) FRANCE

NOTRE-DAME DE PARIS (1831)

During his lifetime, Victor Hugo was known as much as a poet and a dramatist as he was as a novelist but today he is remembered outside France almost solely for his vast, panoramic fiction. *Les Misérables* may be most familiar today in its stage musical adaptation but the book, one of the greatest of all nineteenth-century French novels, demands still to be read. The story of the noble-hearted convict Valjean and his relentless pursuit by the corrupt police inspector Javert opens in the year of Waterloo and culminates in the unsuccessful uprising against monarchical rule that took place in the streets of Paris in June 1832. A year earlier than the date which marks the climax of *Les Misérables*, Hugo, then still a young man in his twenties, published *Notre-Dame de Paris*, most often known in English as *The Hunchback of Notre Dame*. The novel is set in medieval Paris. At its heart is the story of the beautiful foundling Esmeralda, the men who try to seduce her, and Quasimodo, hunchbacked bell-ringer at the cathedral of Notre-Dame, who loves her. Quasimodo was abandoned soon after his birth because of his deformities and only survived because he was taken into the cathedral by Frollo, its archdeacon. He repays Frollo with his devotion but everything changes with the arrival of Esmeralda. The archdeacon becomes obsessed by the gypsy dancer, torn between priestly celibacy and his lust for her. His scheming to possess her results in her entanglement in a murder case and Quasimodo is obliged to rescue her from hanging. He brings her into the sanctuary of the cathedral but there proves to be no way to avoid the tragic fate that awaits all three of them. Melodramatic and highly-coloured, *Notre-Dame de Paris* deserves the fame it has gained from countless stage, film and TV adaptations. It remains one of the most memorable of all historical romances.

Film version: *The Hunchback of Notre Dame* (1939, starring Charles Laughton as Quasimodo)

Read on
Les Misérables; *The Man Who Laughs*
Gustave Flaubert, *Salammbo*; Alessandro Manzoni, *The Betrothed*; Charles Reade, *The Cloister and the Hearth*; ➤➤ Sir Walter Scott, *Quentin Durward*

M.M. KAYE (1908–2004) INDIA/UK

THE FAR PAVILIONS (1978)

The Far Pavilions is an epic romance of the nineteenth-century Raj, set in the decades after the Indian Mutiny and emphasising the ties that bind Britain to her empire. These ties are embodied in the person of Ashton Pelham-Martyn who is born the son of an English scientist and his wife but is brought up, after the deaths of his parents, as a Hindu. In the small kingdom of Gulkote, the boy (known there as Ashok) grows up and meets for the first time the young princess Anjuli. Rediscovering his British heritage when he gets older, Ashton/Ashok becomes an officer in the army in India. While escorting a bridal party across India he encounters Anjuli once more and the passionate love they awaken in one another plunges them both into a web of intrigue and adventure. Mollie Kaye was born into the heart of the Raj she would later memorialise in her best-known book, the daughter of a British linguist and cipher expert in the Indian Civil Service. She had been working on *The Far Pavilions* for more than a decade before it was finally published in 1978 but it was not her first novel. She had been publishing children's stories and detective fiction since the 1930s, and she had also written novels in the 1950s which drew on her knowledge of Indian history. *Shadow of the Moon*, for example, is a highly-charged romance, set in an India ravaged by the Mutiny, and following the love affair between Captain Alex Randall and the improbably-named heiress Winter de Ballesteros. None of these books had gained Kaye the sort of attention and acclaim that came her way with the publication of *The Far Pavilions*. A combination of adventure story and romance on a grand scale, this huge and absorbing saga, a kind of *Gone with the Wind* for the sub-continent, deserved all the many plaudits it received.

🎞 **Film version:** *The Far Pavilions* (1984, TV mini-series)

📚 **Read on**
Shadow of the Moon; *Trade Wind*
Thalassa Ali, *A Singular Hostage*; Valerie Fitzgerald, *Zemindar*; Rebecca Ryman, *Shalimar*; Carolyn Slaughter, *A Black Englishman*

READ ON A THEME: ASIA

Tash Aw, *The Harmony Silk Factory* (Malaysia in the 1930s and 1940s)
Liza Dalby, *The Tale of Murasaki*
Robert Elegant, *Manchu*
Shusaku Endo, *Silence* (Catholic missionaries in seventeenth-century Japan)
Amitav Ghosh, *Sea of Poppies* (set during the Opium Wars)
C.S. Godshalk, *Kalimantaan* (nineteenth-century Borneo)
Arthur Golden, *Memoirs of a Geisha*
Daniel Mason, *The Piano Tuner* (nineteenth-century Burma)
Anchee Min, *Empress Orchid*

THOMAS KENEALLY (b. 1935) AUSTRALIA

THE PLAYMAKER (1987)

Thomas Keneally is best known by far for his novel *Schindler's Ark*, which won the Booker Prize in 1982 and was later adapted into the movie *Schindler's List* by Steven Spielberg, but he has written fiction set in a wide range of places and a variety of historical periods. *The Chant of Jimmie Blacksmith*, for example, is about racial tensions and discrimination reaching a violent conclusion in early 1900s Australia; *Blood Red, Sister Rose* is Keneally's powerful version of the story of Joan of Arc; *Confederates* is a saga of the American Civil War. *The Playmaker* revisits the early years of his own nation, Australia. Plenty of other Australian novelists have turned to the subject of the First and Second Fleets and the convicts transported to New South Wales but Keneally's choice of particular story to tell at the time of Australia's bicentennial is unusual. He focuses on a group of convicts who are engaged in rehearsing and then performing George Farquhar's Restoration comedy *The Recruiting Officer*. Under the guidance of a would-be liberal army lieutenant named Ralph Clark, the prisoners set about bringing to life Farquhar's drama of social and sexual mores in a world they have left far behind them. The difficulties Clark faces as Australia's first theatrical impresario are many and varied – from shortage of scripts to his own confused feelings about one of his actresses – but he remains determined to impose culture on an apparently uncultured land. He will make 'the very first presentation of this or any other play ever performed on this new penal planet, which so far as anyone knew had gone from the beginning of time till now absolutely play-less and theatre-less'. Keneally takes this small and curious episode from the earliest days of white Australia and transforms it into a story that reflects the creation of an entire new society.

⮑ Read on
Blood Red, Sister Rose; *A Victim of the Aurora*
Peter Carey, *True History of the Kelly Gang*

A.L. KENNEDY (b. 1965) UK

DAY (2007)
One of the most distinctive and wholly original voices in British fiction recently has been that of A.L. Kennedy. Kennedy's use of a black, biting humour and vividly original language to explore themes of isolation, emotional impoverishment, sexual passion and love is very powerful and has won her many admirers. Perhaps to the surprise of some of those admirers, in her most recent novel, *Day*, she looked back to the past for her subject matter. The year is 1949 and Alfred Day is in northern Germany, working as an extra in a war film about a POW camp. Forlorn and wretched, surrounded by pretend prisoners, pretend guards, pretend fences, he returns to the bitter experiences of the real war which have made him the damaged man he is. 'You could dodge certain thoughts,' he tells himself, 'corkscrew off and get yourself out of their way, but they'd still hunt you.' Kennedy's novel follows the hunt as Day's thoughts slowly circle their prey. Bit by bit, with great technical

skill, Kennedy unveils Day's history. Scarred by an upbringing dominated by his violent father, he volunteers to join the RAF as means of escape. As a tail-gunner in a Lancaster bomber, he finds his place in the war and, in the desperate camaraderie of his crew, men obliged to live each day with the knowledge that they might not survive to the next, a sense of belonging he has never possessed before. After a chance meeting during a London air raid, he also finds love. All that he gains, he loses as the war continues. Broken and traumatised, he ends up in the kind of encampment the film-makers struggle to recreate a few years later. *Day* is a brilliant reconstruction of the recent past and a fascinating portrait of a man whose war has rendered him unfit for peace.

🐟 Read on

Ian McEwan, *Atonement*; Sarah Waters, *The Night Watch*

CHARLES KINGSLEY (1819–75) UK

WESTWARD HO! (1855)

Charles Kingsley was a clergyman and Christian Socialist who became professor of Modern History at Cambridge. Today he is best remembered for *The Water-Babies*, a children's book in which a mistreated chimney sweep's boy runs away from his master and is transformed into a water-baby. In his own lifetime he was famous for novels of social concern, like *Alton Locke*, and for historical fiction. *Hypatia* is a story set in fifth-century Alexandria; *Hereward the Wake* follows the adventures of an Anglo-Saxon warrior, the 'Last of the English', as he battles with doomed heroism against the invading Normans under the command of William the Conqueror. Of Kingsley's novels set in the past, the liveliest and most interesting is *Westward Ho!* Set in Elizabethan Devonshire, it follows the adventures of Amyas Leigh as he sets sail with Drake and other privateers of the age to smite the Spaniards in the Caribbean. Amyas grows up in Bideford and dreams from an early age of adventures at sea. Thwarted in his love for the beautiful Rose Salterne, he sails for Ireland where he captures a Spanish nobleman, Don Guzman, and brings him back to his home port. The treacherous Don immediately sets about seducing Rose and she flees with him to the Indies. The stage is set for Amyas and his brother Frank (another of Rose's admirers) to mount an expedition to the Caribbean to rescue her. As Kingsley's long and involved plot unfolds, tragedy lurks in the wings and Amyas is destined to be transformed into a man intent on little but revenge for the losses he suffers. *Westward Ho!* is a novel that is very much of its time. Its virulent anti-Catholicism and its attitude towards native peoples – an unappealing mixture of bigotry and condescension – make some of it difficult reading today. Yet the book has a vitality that makes it well worth overlooking the worst of its shortcomings.

🐾 Read on
Hereward the Wake; *Hypatia*
R.D. Blackmore, *Lorna Doone*; H. Rider Haggard, *Montezuma's Daughter*

MATTHEW KNEALE (b. 1960) UK

ENGLISH PASSENGERS (2000)

Matthew Kneale is the son of two writers (Nigel Kneale, creator of Professor Quatermass for a 1950s BBC TV series, and the children's author Judith Kerr) and began to publish his own fiction soon after graduating from Oxford. He has written two of the most vivid and unusual historical novels of the last twenty years. *Sweet Thames* is set in Victorian London and may well be the only work of fiction ever written to have a sewage engineer as its hero. Joshua Jeavons, a character loosely based on the real-life Sir Joseph Bazalgette, is a visionary who dreams of a future city cleansed of filth and disease but he is forced into a quest through the grubby nether world of the real London by the mysterious disappearance of his wife. *English Passengers*, set like its predecessor in the Victorian era, weaves together many narrative voices to tell the story of an ill-fated voyage to Tasmania in the 1850s. The Reverend Geoffrey Wilson is a fundamentalist clergyman determined to trump pretentious scientists by discovering the Garden of Eden in the southern hemisphere and thus proving the literal truth of the Bible. Accompanying him on his quixotic mission are a surgeon out to gain evidence for his own contentious theory of man's origins and a shipload of Manx smugglers who have agreed to transport the expedition southwards for devious reasons of their own. Most ambitiously, one of the twenty different voices in which Kneale tells his story is that of Peevay, a Tasmanian Aborigine, and his account is not one of Eden rediscovered but of a people and a culture brutally destroyed. Kneale creates a narrative tour de force in *English Passengers*, weaving together its many different strands into a coherent whole and producing a tale that confronts the cruel realities of the colonial past.

🐞 Read on

Sweet Thames

>> Robert Edric, *Elysium*; Harry Thompson, *This Thing of Darkness*

JAAN KROSS (1920–2007) ESTONIA

THE CZAR'S MADMAN (1978)

Jaan Kross was the most widely translated and internationally best-known Estonian writer of the twentieth century. Much of his work can be classified as historical fiction. *Professor Martens' Departure*, for example, takes as its central character a real-life Estonian academic and diplomat from the nineteenth century and reveals his innermost thoughts about his life and times as he makes a final train journey from his home town to St Petersburg. It can be argued that it was only through looking back into the nineteenth century that Kross found a way to throw light obliquely on the trials and travails of his nation in the more recent past. Not all of Kross's work has been translated into English but, of the books that have, the finest is probably *The Czar's Madman*. The title character is an early nineteenth-century Estonian nobleman, Baron Timotheus von Bock, an idealist who believes in the equality of men and makes the mistake of assuming that the Czar will listen to him when he tells him of the injustices in his realm. (Estonia was then part of the Russian Empire.) He writes a letter to the Czar making his criticisms plain. Far from listening, the Czar assumes that von Bock is insane and has him incarcerated for nine years. The story is told by Jakob, von Bock's brother-in-law, whose sister Eeva the Baron marries in defiance of convention and their difference in social status. In his journal, Jakob puzzles over the question of his brother-in-law's character. Is he a madman, as the Czar thought, and as current society judges him, or is he a heroic exemplar of a better way of living? The hints of parallels between von Bock's fate and those of the victims of a more recent and brutal absolutism are clear but *The Czar's Madman* also triumphs as a moving portrait of a man whose saintly idealism is thwarted by the realities of the society in which he lives.

🕮 Read on

Professor Martens' Departure
Per Olov Enquist, *The Visit of the Royal Physician*

GIUSEPPE TOMASI DI LAMPEDUSA
(1896–1957) ITALY

THE LEOPARD (1958)

Giuseppe Tomasi, 11th Prince of Lampedusa, was born in Palermo, a member of the old Sicilian nobility, and was educated there and in Rome. Apart from service in the Italian army as a young man during the First World War, Lampedusa lived a life that was largely devoid of external incident. He read, he travelled, he led the existence of a literary dilettante. *The Leopard* was his only novel and it was published posthumously, although he had had the first ideas about the work when he was still in his twenties. It tells the story of a Sicilian aristocrat, Prince Fabrizio de Salina, and his family, and their experiences during the revolutionary upheavals surrounding the Unification of Italy in the nineteenth century. The novel opens in May 1860 and Garibaldi, hero of the unification movement, has just landed with his army of 'redshirts' on the coast of Sicily. The Prince, proud and sensual, continues to hold what is close to feudal power over his estates and he assumes a benevolent despotism when it comes to the affairs of his extended family. Change, however, is inevitable. Garibaldi, although he never appears directly in the book, is a powerful offstage presence and it is clear that the new Sicily that follows him will not be the one that the Prince knows. His favourite nephew Tancredi welcomes the Risorgimento and remarks to his uncle, in the most famous line in the book, 'If we want things to stay as they are, things will have to change'. The Prince, however, cannot change and the book follows his melancholic realisation that he is out of step with the times. Slow-moving and leisurely, *The Leopard* is not a novel for those seeking action-packed narrative. For those readers who admire beautiful prose, the subtle delineation of character and an authorial voice that is detached, ironic and wise, Lampedusa's solitary masterpiece may be just the book for them.

🐚 Read on

Giorgio Bassani, *The Garden of the Finzi-Continis*; Leonardo Sciascia, *The Council of Egypt*

AMIN MAALOUF (b. 1949) LEBANON/FRANCE

BALTHASAR'S ODYSSEY (2002)

Maalouf was born in Beirut and lived there until 1975 when the civil war in Lebanon drove him into exile. He went to Paris and it was in France and in French that he began to publish fiction. One of his early novels, *Rock of Tanios*, won the Prix Goncourt, France's major prize for fiction, in 1993. Like Maalouf himself, many of the protagonists of his fiction are wanderers or exiles and this is certainly true of Balthasar Embriaco, the central character in *Balthasar's Odyssey*. This picaresque novel, first published in French in the millennial year of 2000, takes another potentially apocalyptic year for its historical setting. As 1666, the Year of the Beast, approaches, Balthasar, an Italian merchant in the Levant, briefly takes possession of a book (a religious text containing the hidden Hundredth Name of God) that might have the power to avert any impending disasters. Balthasar's regret after trading the book prompts him to go in search of it. Accompanied by his two nephews, the scholarly Jaber and the more worldly Habib, and by a deserted wife named Marta, who is aiming to gain legal proof that her husband's prolonged absence means she is a widow, he sets off from his home town on what becomes a long and arduous journey. They travel first to the vast, imperial metropolis of Constantinople and then on to Smyrna, where he becomes involved in the religious revivalism surrounding the self-styled Jewish messiah Sabbatai Zvi. Eventually Balthasar's travels take him as far as London at the time of the Great Fire. Throughout the novel, Embriaco is a man torn between reason and faith. He is sceptical about the power of the book he has had and lost but he is still prepared to journey halfway around the known world in order to retrieve it. He becomes the engaging hero of a narrative that celebrates the diversity of a vanished Mediterranean world where Islamic and Christian cultures met and interacted.

🐚 Read on

Leo the African

Tariq Ali, *Shadows of the Pomegranate Tree*; ›› Geraldine Brooks, *People of the Book*; Robert Irwin, *The Arabian Nightmare*; Bernice Rubens, *Kingdom Come* (a novel about Sabbatai Zvi)

HILARY MANTEL (b. 1952) UK

A PLACE OF GREATER SAFETY (1992)

Hilary Mantel's fiction has ranged from a story of expatriates in Saudi Arabia struggling to make sense of the claustrophobic and alien society in which they find themselves (*Eight Months on Ghazzah Street*) to a darkly comic tale of a medium haunted by visions of the past as well as the future (*Beyond Black*). However, her first attempt at narrative was a historical novel. She began what became *A Place of Greater Safety* soon after leaving university. Rejected by a publisher, it was put aside for many years and only re-emerged after Mantel had written and published several other works of fiction. The novel is set during the French Revolution and takes the revolutionary leaders Danton, Robespierre and Camille Desmoulins as its central characters. Mantel blends recorded facts with her own inventions to reconstruct the early lives of the three men and then follows them from the provinces to Paris, through the heady first days of the Revolution, the intricate political manoeuvrings and the Terror, to their eventual deaths by guillotine. It takes ambition to pick a subject as huge as the French Revolution as the basis for your fiction but Mantel succeeds brilliantly in conveying the electric excitement and sense of potential that fuelled it, and her portrait of the complicated, triangular relationship between her three main figures is entirely convincing. Her most recent book, *Wolf Hall*, is a rich reconstruction of the power struggles of Tudor London but this earlier novel was already exploring the territory where politics and the individual clash nearly twenty years ago. *A Place of Greater Safety* thrusts its readers headlong into the tumult and bloodshed of France as the world of the *ancien régime* is turned upside down and her characters battle to create a new society that can successfully replace the old.

🥢 Read on

The Giant, O'Brien; *Wolf Hall*

Helen Dunmore, *The Siege*; Thomas Flanagan, *The Year of the French*; Tanith Lee, *The Gods Are Thirsty*; Marge Piercy, *City of Darkness, City of Light*

JOHN MASTERS (1914–83) UK

NIGHTRUNNERS OF BENGAL (1951)

John Masters was born into an army family that had a tradition of service in India stretching back several generations. He served the Raj as a soldier himself and, when he retired and took up writing, it was unsurprising that he should draw upon the history of British India for his stories. Nearly all his fiction is set in India and seven of his novels tell the tales of members of successive generations of one particular family in the country, the Savages. Perhaps the best of these is *Nightrunners of Bengal*, set at the time of the Indian Mutiny. The protagonist of the novel is Captain Rodney Savage of the Bengal Infantry who is serving in an isolated garrison in the heart of India at the beginning of the fateful year of 1857. As Masters's narrative unfolds, Savage sees the garrison fall to rebellious sepoys and his wife killed in the violence. Escaping the massacres with his infant son and a young Englishwoman named Caroline Langford, he takes shelter with villagers loyal to British rule and must look for ways to survive and reconstruct his life.

In the thirty-two years between the publication of *Nightrunners of Bengal* and his death, Masters produced nearly twenty more novels, ranging from *The Deceivers*, which tells the story of Rodney Savage's father and his attempts to infiltrate and destroy the cult of assassins known as the Thuggee, to *The Ravi Lancers*, a tale of an Indian regiment sent to fight on the Western Front in the First World War. His fiction has sometimes been criticised as too overtly pro-British and it is true that Masters admired the Raj his family served for so long. However, his work was more open-minded and generous than his critics allow. A book like *Nightrunners of Bengal* may seem dated in its sympathies today but its virtues – compelling readability and imaginative recreation of the past – are undeniable.

🕮 Read on

The Deceivers; *The Lotus and the Wind*
>> Bernard Cornwell, *Sharpe's Tiger*; Allan Mallinson, *The Nizam's Daughters* (more recently published adventures stories set in the Raj)

COLLEEN MCCULLOUGH (b. 1937) AUSTRALIA

THE FIRST MAN IN ROME (1990)

Before the publication of *The First Man in Rome*, Colleen McCullough was best known for *The Thornbirds*, a best-selling saga of life in the Australian outback which was also made into a successful TV series. A meticulous reconstruction of the political life of Ancient Rome must have seemed an unlikely project for her as a novelist but, over seventeen years and seven volumes of the 'Masters of Rome' series, she carried it off with enormous vision and panache. In *The First Man in Rome*, the first of a sequence which charts the transition of the Roman state from a republic to an empire, the focus is on the years when the giants of the late republic, Marius and Sulla, vie for power. The two men are contrasting figures – Marius a low-born pleb who has risen to great heights and Sulla a patrician struggling to maintain his status in the world – but McCullough creates thoroughly convincing portraits of them both. And she sets their rivalry (and occasional collaborations) amidst the pullulating life of Rome at the time. She marshals the twists and turns of the politics and the personal relationships into a coherent narrative and handles the lengthy cast list of characters with great aplomb. Nearly a thousand pages long, *The First Man in Rome* is none the less only an introduction to the full series which carries the story forwards to the campaigns of Pompey the Great (*Fortune's Favourites*), the rise of Caesar (*Caesar*) and, finally, the last great confrontation between Mark Antony and Octavian (*Antony and Cleopatra*). With the family sagas with which she started her career, Colleen McCullough proved herself a storyteller of remarkable gifts. When she directed these gifts to the recreation of some of the most dramatic events in the history of ancient Rome, she produced a very different but no less enthralling kind of fiction.

⮑ Read on

The Grass Crown; *Fortune's Favourites* (and others in the 'Masters of Rome series)

Gillian Bradshaw, *Cleopatra's Heir*; Alfred Duggan, *Three's Company*; Howard Fast, *Spartacus* (the story of the famous slave revolt in ancient Rome as told by a left-wing American novelist)

JAMES MEEK (b. 1962) UK

THE PEOPLE'S ACT OF LOVE (2005)

James Meek worked for many years as a journalist and lived as a foreign correspondent in Kiev and Moscow for most of the 1990s. His third novel, *The People's Act of Love*, is set in Russia during the years of upheaval that followed the Bolshevik Revolution. The events of the book take place in a remote part of Siberia but even here the violence and turmoil of the larger world obtrude. Somewhere over the horizon of the bleak landscape, the civil war between the Red armies of the Bolsheviks and the White armies of the Tsarists is under way. The small township of Yazyk is under martial law but its rulers are not Russian.

They are the survivors of a regiment of Czech soldiers, unwilling conscripts against the Bolsheviks, who have been stranded in the wastelands of the far north. Led by their deranged commander, Captain Matula, the Czechs terrorise the people of Yazyk, members of a strange Christian sect, yet long only to escape from their frozen exile. Into this trapped community comes a charismatic man called Samarin, claiming to be a revolutionary who has fled from one of the Tsar's gulags. His arrival triggers a sequence of violent events which engulf every character in the novel from Matula and Samarin to Lieutenant Mutz, a humane Czech officer plotting to escape Matula's megalomaniac tyranny, Balashov, the enigmatic leader of the sect, and Anna Petrovna, a young widow whose past contains disturbing secrets. *The People's Act of Love* is one of the most memorable and original historical novels of recent years. It works brilliantly both as a narrative that grips the imagination from its start and as an unflinching analysis of the ways in which utopian dreams spiral out of control and end as nightmares of oppression and inhumanity.

☙ Read on

Robert Alexander, *The Kitchen Boy*; Ken Kalfus, *The Commissariat of Enlightenment*

NAOMI MITCHISON (1897–1999) UK

THE CORN KING AND THE SPRING QUEEN (1931)

The daughter of the physiologist John Scott Haldane and the sister of the well-known scientist J.B.S. Haldane, Naomi Mitchison came from a Scottish family that was at the heart of British intellectual life for much of the twentieth century. In the course of her own exceptionally long life she published plays, memoirs, poetry and more than fifty novels. Mitchison's very first novel, *The Conquered*, which was published in 1923, took its subject from the distant past (Gaul at the time of Julius Caesar's invasions) and much of her best fiction was historical. Settings for her novels ranged from Scotland in the aftermath of the Jacobite Rising of 1745 (*The Bull Calves*) to Classical Greece (*Cloud Cuckoo Land*) but her most original book is *The Corn King and the Spring Queen* which brilliantly mixes history and mythology. The Spring Queen of the title is Erif Der. The book opens in Erif's own land, Marob, which lies on the shores of the Black Sea. There Erif and her consort Tarrik are the ritual leaders of the community whose magical powers ensure fertility for the land and food for the people. When Erif, taking Tarrik's side against that of her father, is punished by the death of her first-born, she takes a revenge that forces her to leave her native country. Bereft of her magic, she travels first to Greece and then to Egypt, searching for redemption and renewal of her powers. With its sense of the supernatural rooted in the natural world and its clever reworking of imagery and ideas taken from J.G. Frazer's pioneering anthropological studies of mystery religions, *The Corn King and the Spring Queen* is a strange and wonderful novel. Elements of historical fiction, fantasy fiction and feminist reworking of ancient myths all come together to create a unique concoction.

🐚 Read on

The Blood of the Martyrs; *The Bull Calves*

Margaret Elphinstone, *The Gathering Night*; Ursula K. Le Guin, *Lavinia*

LAWRENCE NORFOLK (b. 1963) UK

THE POPE'S RHINOCEROS (1996)

Lawrence Norfolk has a high reputation as a novelist but it rests on a small body of work. He has published only three novels in nearly twenty years. His first book, *Lemprière's Dictionary*, which takes as its starting point the life of the eighteenth-century classical scholar John Lemprière, was published in 1991 and won him a place on the 1993 Granta Best of Young British Novelists list. *The Pope's Rhinoceros* appeared three years later. The novel, like its predecessor, is a long narrative that raids both history and legend in search of stories to entertain and educate the reader. It is set in the sixteenth century. A new world has been discovered across the Atlantic and two great maritime powers – Spain and Portugal – are competing to gain a monopoly of its riches. In Rome, the pope holds the key to the division of the spoils. That pope is Leo X, a man with an obsessive interest in the collection of marvels and prodigies from around a world that is rapidly expanding as Europeans journey into the *terra incognita* of other continents. Leo has an elephant but he has read of even stranger beasts in classical literature and he yearns to add them to his menagerie. Representatives of Spain and Portugal enter a race to provide the pope with what he wants. The book's heroes are two archetypally picaresque characters, Salvestro and Bernardo, who are eventually duped into heading for West Africa in an attempt to satisfy the pope's zoological whim. However, the search for the 'Beast' (never named as a rhinoceros save in the book's title) is only the most important of many hooks from which Norfolk hangs a motley collection of tall traveller's tales. He is a writer who believes in giving readers quantity as much as quality and his second novel is a flamboyant ragbag of digressions, displays of offbeat erudition and stories within stories.

🕮 Read on

Lemprière's Dictionary
T. Coraghessan Boyle, *Water Music*; Thomas Pynchon, *Mason & Dixon*; Neal Stephenson, *Quicksilver*

PATRICK O'BRIAN (1914–2000) UK

MASTER AND COMMANDER (1969)

Patrick O'Brian's Jack Aubrey novels, about an officer in the British Navy in Napoleonic times, chart his hero's progress up the ranks and place him amidst many of the great events of the era. *Master and Commander* is the first in the series, set in the year 1800, and records the first meeting between Aubrey, at this point a lowly lieutenant in the Royal Navy, and Stephen Maturin, a half-Irish, half-Catalan ship's surgeon and naturalist. The friendship between the two of them is at the heart of the series but it gets off to a bad start. At a concert in Port Mahon, Minorca, they nearly come to blows when Maturin reprimands Aubrey for beating time and humming to the music. The damage is soon repaired and the two men, contrasting characters though they are, come to like one another. When Aubrey, promoted to Commander and in charge of the sloop *Sophie*, discovers that he needs a ship's surgeon, he invites Maturin to take the position. As the *Sophie* cruises the Mediterranean in search of potential French and Spanish prizes, and as the dangers of the war at sea become all too real, the previously landlubbing Maturin is introduced to the world of the Royal Navy. In the books that followed *Master and Commander*, O'Brian despatched the two friends around the world in a series of adventures from the East Indies (*HMS Surprise*) to Chile (*Blue at the Mizzen*) via the Greek Islands (*The Ionian Mission*) and the penal settlements of New South Wales (*The Nutmeg of Consolation*). Admirers of the books often run out of superlatives when they are describing them. In the range of research and the skill with which the knowledge gained is deployed, in the depth of characterisation, particularly of the two main protagonists, in the drama of the storytelling, the Aubrey novels are unsurpassed.

🖝 Film version: *Master and Commander* (2003, starring Russell Crowe as Jack Aubrey and Paul Bettany as Stephen Maturin and taking its title if not much of its plot from the first novel)

🥢 Read on
Post Captain; *HMS Surprise*; *The Mauritius Command* (and the seventeen further books in the 'Aubrey/Maturin' series)
>> C.S. Forester, *The Gun*; Alexander Kent, *Richard Bolitho, Midshipman*

JOSEPH O'CONNOR (b. 1963) IRELAND

REDEMPTION FALLS (2007)

The Star of the Sea, a gripping novel in which refugees from the disaster of the Irish Potato Famine of the 1840s flee their ravaged native land for the hope and promise of the New World, won both critical and commercial success when it was first published in 2002. Its author was the Dublin-born writer Joseph O'Connor. Five years later, O'Connor published *Redemption Falls*, an even more ambitious story of the Irish in America. There are tenuous links between the two books (the later novel opens as the daughter of two of the passengers from *The Star of the Sea* embarks on a long walk across America in search of her missing brother) but the focus in *Redemption Falls* is firmly on the new land rather than the old. James Con O'Keeffe is a former hero of the nationalist struggle against the British, an escapee from the convict colonies of Tasmania who became first a celebrity in the USA and then a flamboyant Union general in the American Civil War. Now, the war over, he is drowning in whisky and self-recrimination in the frontier town of Redemption Falls. His wife Lucia, neglected and frustrated, turns to an unlikely admirer in a disfigured cartographer sent to map the region. As O'Keeffe bestirs himself to pursue the vigilantes and outlaws who make the land wretched and becomes obsessed by a mute boy who pitches up in the town, the stage is set for tragedy. O'Connor makes brilliant use of all kinds of material – letters, journals, folk ballads, transcripts of court proceedings, even wanted posters – to tell the story of O'Keeffe and those whose lives he overturns and transforms. Avoiding the predictability of linear narrative, O'Connor creates a multi-layered story which continues to provide surprises until its final, revelatory few words.

🦑 Read on

Star of the Sea
Peter Behrens, *The Law of Dreams*; Liam O'Flaherty, *Famine*; Michael White, *Soul Catcher*

BARONESS EMMA ORCZY (1865–1947)
HUNGARY/UK

THE SCARLET PIMPERNEL (1905)

Born in Budapest, Emmuska Orczy moved with her parents to England as a young girl. She studied at art schools in London, where she met her husband, and her first published works were versions of Hungarian fairy tales which she translated and he illustrated. Her first historical novel appeared at the end of the 1890s, as did her first detective story, and it was into those two genres that nearly all her later work fitted. Much her most famous creation is *The Scarlet Pimpernel* which was originally a drama on the London stage. The play, and the novel that swiftly followed, introduced one of the more enduring figures in popular historical fiction in Sir Percy Blakeney. Blakeney is an apparently effete Englishman who, in reality, is none other than the Scarlet Pimpernel, the daring and mysterious saviour of French aristocrats from the Revolutionary guillotine. In the first book of what became a long-running series, the elusive Pimpernel is the talk of London and a man admired by everyone in society, including Marguerite, the French-born wife of the foppish English gentleman, Sir Percy Blakeney. Marguerite has problems in plenty. Estranged from her husband, whom she has come to regard with contempt, she is being blackmailed by the French envoy Chauvelin who holds the fate of her brother Armand in his hands. In exchange for the life of Armand, still trapped in Revolutionary France, she provides Chauvelin with information that leads him to the true identity of the Pimpernel. Too late Marguerite discovers that the hero of the hour is actually the husband she despised and that, since he has recently crossed the Channel, she has unwittingly placed him in terrible danger. She must follow him to Paris to save him from Chauvelin and his minions. *The Scarlet Pimpernel* may now seem dated in its language and improbable in its plotting but it retains an uncomplicated vitality that continues to attract readers today.

◣ **Film versions:** *The Scarlet Pimpernel* (1934, starring Leslie Howard as the Pimpernel); *The Scarlet Pimpernel* (1999, TV series starring Richard E. Grant in the title role)

▽ **Read on**
I Will Repay; *The Elusive Pimpernel* (the earliest two of the many Scarlet Pimpernel novels Baroness Orczy published during her life); *Beau Brocade* (set at the time of Bonnie Prince Charlie)
Jeffery Farnol, *The Amateur Gentleman*; ▸▸ Rafael Sabatini, *Scaramouche: A Romance of the French Revolution*

CHARLES PALLISER (b. 1947) US/UK

THE UNBURIED (1999)

An American academic who has spent much of his life in Britain, Charles Palliser is best known for *The Quincunx*, published in 1989. In this epic imitation of the high Victorian novel a young man named John Huffam pursues the complex truth about his family history and a legal document which has shaped his own life and the lives of most of the characters in the book. A decade later, Palliser published *The Unburied*, a shorter but no less skilfully confected novel which drew on late Victorian genre fiction and the work of Edwardian masters of the ghost story like M.R. James to create a narrative to baffle and entertain readers. 'While my memory is fresh,' the novel begins, 'I am going to describe exactly what I saw and heard on the occasion, less than a week past, when I encountered a man who was walking about just like you and me – despite the inconvenience of having been brutally done to death.' The narrator who provides this attention-grabbing opening is Edward Courtine, a historian who travels to the fictional English cathedral town of Thurchester to pursue his researches into the life and times of Alfred the Great in the cathedral library. Instead of the antiquarian investigations of manuscripts and parchments he is expecting, he finds himself drawn into two mysteries. One is from the past – a macabre tale of ghosts and murder told to him by his host, an old college friend he has not seen for years. The other, very much in the present, is a brutal killing that shocks the quiet cathedral town. As the two intertwine, Courtine, a witness in the recent murder, struggles to make sense of what he has seen and read and heard. In *The Unburied*, Palliser slowly unveils a fiendishly complicated plot and, in doing so, produces a small masterpiece of historical suspense.

≋ Read on

The Quincunx

John Maclachlan Gray, *The Fiend in Human*; John Harwood, *The Séance*; Dan Simmons, *Drood*

ORHAN PAMUK (b. 1952) TURKEY

MY NAME IS RED (1998)

Orhan Pamuk, winner of the Nobel Prize for Literature in 2006, is Turkey's most famous writer. He has published a number of best-selling novels and a memoir of growing up in Istanbul, the city that has shaped his imagination. 'Istanbul's fate,' he has written, 'is my fate: I am attached to this city because it has made me who I am.' Like his memoir, his finest fiction draws on the peculiar history of his native city. *The White Castle* is set in the seventeenth century and traces the relationship between two scholars, one a Turkish savant living in Constantinople, the other a Venetian captured and sold to him as a slave. The two men resemble one another physically and Pamuk uses this similarity as a metaphor to explore the intermingling of east and west that characterises Turkish culture past and present. *My Name Is Red*, however, is his most powerful reconstruction of the past. In this complex and subtle novel, the murder of a miniaturist, engaged to produce a magnificently illuminated book for a sixteenth-century Sultan, is the starting point for a narrative that is partly a kind of detective story and partly an investigation into the interconnections between love and art and power. The artists who work on the Sultan's book are not only caught up in the mystery of who killed their colleague. They are also at the heart of a debate about the nature of art itself – should it continue to follow the ancient traditions of the East or adopt the new techniques of the West? – and they are threatened by the Machiavellian plotting and jostling for position that surrounds the ruler. The central character in the narrative, known only as Black, is torn between conflicting loyalties and made miserable by his love for his beautiful cousin. Using short chapters and a miscellany of often unlikely narrators, Pamuk builds up an extraordinary portrait of a past culture.

📖 Read on

The White Castle

Jason Goodwin, *The Janissary Tree*; Katie Hickman, *The Aviary Gate* (two very different novels set in Constantinople); Kunal Basu, *The Miniaturist*; Ismail Kadare, *The Siege*

MATTHEW PEARL USA

THE DANTE CLUB (2003)

A serial killer is stalking the streets of Boston in the year 1865. His victims meet terrible and bizarre deaths. A judge is struck on the head and left to be eaten alive by maggots. A church minister is buried upside-down in a pit and his feet set on fire. Only a small group of poets and scholars, including such famous men as Henry Wadsworth Longfellow and Oliver Wendell Holmes, recognise a method in the killer's apparent madness. Devotees of the Italian poet Dante (whose *Divine Comedy* Longfellow is translating into English), they realise that the killer is modelling his murders on the descriptions of hell's punishments in their idol's works and they must set about bringing him to justice. However, as the Dante Club members begin to unravel the mystery and move slowly towards the unmasking of the murderer's identity, he turns his attention to them. He has his own peculiar obsession with their work and his own strange way of demonstrating a devotion to Dante. The bookish Bostonians are obliged to think and act quickly to save themselves and others from a psychopath intent on pursuing his delusions to the bitter end. *The Dante Club* has been a great success with both readers and critics and Matthew Pearl has followed it with another tale of nineteenth-century literary mystery. In *The Poe Shadow* an admirer of the author of *Tales of Mystery and Imagination* decides that the one person to investigate the circumstances surrounding his tragic death is the person on whom Poe modelled his famous fictional detective, C. Auguste Dupin. Problems arise when two candidates for the inspirational role make their separate claims. In both these novels, Matthew Pearl has revealed a talent for combining erudition, historical detail and devious plotting to great effect.

🕮 Read on

The Poe Shadow; *The Last Dickens*
Tony Pollard, *The Minutes of the Lazarus Club*; Jed Rubenfeld, *The Interpretation of Murder*

IAIN PEARS (b. 1955)

AN INSTANCE OF THE FINGERPOST (1997)

An art historian who began his career as a novelist writing detective stories set in the art world, Iain Pears became an international bestseller with the publication of *An Instance of the Fingerpost*, a book which is a clever combination of intellectual whodunit and historical novel. The year is 1663 and Dr Robert Grove is found dead, presumed poisoned, in his room in New College, Oxford. A chambermaid, Sarah Blundy, is accused of the crime and confesses her guilt but did she really kill Grove? Four different narrators give their own versions of events and the truth slowly emerges from a swirling mass of contradictions and red-herrings. The first two to tell their stories – Marco da Cola, a physician visiting Oxford from Venice, and Jack Prescott, a student with a questionable past – are fictional characters but, for his third and last narrators, Pears makes use of real-life characters. John Wallis was a mathematician and cryptographer who, in telling his part of the novel, reveals himself as a paranoid and self-righteous man, forever detecting crime and conspiracy in the world around him; Anthony Wood, known to posterity as a gossipy diarist of Oxford life, is the narrator of the book's fourth section in which the real truth about the events swims into view at last. The curious title of Pears's novel is a reference to words by the philosopher and politician Francis Bacon. In Bacon's philosophy, an 'instance of the fingerpost' is a moment when the fallacies that beset logical thinking fall by the wayside and a marker points unmistakeably to the truth. Pears's narrative takes its readers on an absorbing journey through falsehood, confusion and conflicting ideas about the nature of truth before the fingerpost finally emerges from the darkness and points the way towards a resolution of the mystery.

🕮 Read on
The Dream of Scipio; *Stone's Fall*
➤➤ Robert Edric, *The Earth Made of Glass*; Philip Kerr, *Dark Matter* (Sir Isaac Newton investigates a series of murders in late seventeenth-century London)

SHARON KAY PENMAN (b. 1945) USA

THE SUNNE IN SPLENDOUR (1982)

Was Richard III the hunchbacked villain portrayed by Shakespeare or was he a good man betrayed by those he trusted during his lifetime and traduced by historians ever since? The American historical novelist Sharon Kay Penman has no doubt that Richard has been much-maligned. The king she portrays in *The Sunne in Splendour*, her debut novel, is a man undone by his own virtues. The story she tells, tracing Richard's journey from boyhood to the kingship and (ultimately) to defeat and death at Bosworth Field, is a familiar one but she gives it her own spin. The Richard of her novel is a complex man but a good one. He is loyal to his older brother Edward, the charismatic warrior who seizes the throne of England during the Wars of the Roses, and devotes himself to the Yorkist cause in the North. He is faithful to Anne Neville, the woman he loves above all others, even when it seems she cannot be his wife. Thrust into a role he never wanted, he struggles to be the king that England needs. And, when the time comes to face his death, he does so with courage and dignity. Across more than nine hundred colourful pages, Sharon Kay Penman builds up a picture of Good King Richard to set against the relentless bad press he has received over the centuries. Since publishing *The Sunne in Splendour*, she has had a productive career as a historical novelist. Her books have ranged from an epic set during the civil war in England between King Stephen and the Empress Maude (*When Christ and his Saints Slept*) to a series of medieval whodunnits featuring one Justin de Quincy, trusted servant to Eleanor of Aquitaine. However, her absorbing narrative of the life of England's most controversial king remains the best of her many novels.

🕮 Read on

When Christ and his Saints Slept

Rosemary Hawley Jarman, *We Speak No Treason*; Reay Tannahill, *The Seventh Son* (two further novels with Richard III as their focus)

ARTURO PEREZ-REVERTE (b. 1951) SPAIN

THE FENCING MASTER (1988)

In Spain, Perez-Reverte is most famous for his creation of Captain Alatriste, the daring seventeenth-century swordsman whose adventures are chronicled in a sequence of novels which brilliantly re-work the romances of writers like Dumas for our own, more cynical times. In the rest of the world, he is better known for intellectual thrillers which combine action and page-turning readability with offbeat erudition and intellectual puzzles. In *The Dumas Club*, book-hunter Lucas Corso is dragged into a plot involving murder, sex and obsessive bibliophiles when he is asked to authenticate what looks to be a handwritten chapter from ❯❯ Dumas's adventure story *The Three Musketeers*. *The Flanders Panel* presents the reader with a murder mystery in the art world of modern Madrid which may well depend for its solution on a late medieval painting of a game of chess. *The Fencing Master* is also set in Madrid but it travels back into the past to the eve of the 1868 Revolution which deposed the reactionary Queen Isabella II. It tells the story of Jaime Astarloa, the fencing master of the title, who is drawn against his will into political and erotic intrigue when a young woman knocks on his door and asks to be taught his art. Astarloa is a man of old-fashioned honour and chivalry who feels lost in a modern world which increasingly finds everything he most cherishes either irrelevant or faintly ludicrous. Where others spend their days in fevered discussion of the political changes that are about to overtake the country, Astarloa despises politics and politicians and cares only for the perfection of his swordsmanship and his search for an unstoppable thrust that no fencer can parry. Yet, when he agrees to take on the mysterious Adela de Otero as a pupil, he is dragged into a mire of deceit, betrayal and assassination. Exciting and melancholy in equal measure, Perez-Reverte's story of an honourable man in dishonourable times is one of his finest works.

🕮 Read on

Captain Alatriste (first in the series of novels about a Spanish soldier in seventeenth-century Europe)

Michael Chabon, *Gentlemen of the Road* (a knowing reinvention of old-fashioned swashbuckling fiction that is reminiscent of some of Perez-Reverte's books); Manuel Rivas, *The Carpenter's Pencil*

ELLIS PETERS (1913–95) UK

A MORBID TASTE FOR BONES (1977)

In a career that lasted more than fifty years, Edith Pargeter wrote dozens of crime novels, many of them set in the past. Some were published under her own name and some under pseudonyms, most notably Ellis Peters. Her greatest creation was the humane and sympathetic medieval monk Brother Cadfael who uses his knowledge of herbal medicines and his insights into the mysteries of human motivation to unravel the crimes that come regularly to trouble the town of

Shrewsbury and its monastery. He appears in twenty novels and a number of short stories. In the first in the series, *A Morbid Taste for Bones*, Cadfael is despatched by his abbot to a remote Welsh village where the relics of a saint are held. The abbot's wish is to purchase St Winifred's bones and install them in the monastery in Shrewsbury. The villagers are divided about the wisdom of this plan. Some welcome it; others are vehemently against it. When the leader of the opposition to moving the bones is found murdered, Cadfael needs all his wisdom and intelligence to work out who has killed him and why. *A Morbid Taste for Bones* immediately established the monk from Shrewsbury as one of the most intriguing of historical detectives and his character grew ever more complex as the series continued. TV films featuring Derek Jacobi as Cadfael only confirmed his appeal. Unlike the protagonists of so many series of historical mysteries, the herbalist monk has genuine depth. Ellis Peters provides him with a personal history – he was a soldier in the Crusades before he took the cowl in middle age – and his character has been shaped by a knowledge of the world outside the abbey walls. Many more medieval detectives have flitted through the pages of historical mysteries in the thirty years since *A Morbid Taste for Bones* was published but none has ever really matched him.

▄ Film version: *A Morbid Taste for Bones* (1996, episode of TV series featuring Derek Jacobi as Cadfael)

➥ Read on

One Corpse Too Many; *Monk's Hood* (and a further seventeen titles in the 'Brother Cadfael' series)

Paul Harding (P.C. Doherty), *The Nightingale Gallery*; Candace Robb, *The Apothecary Rose*; Peter Tremayne, *Absolution by Murder*

CARYL PHILLIPS (b. 1958) UK

CAMBRIDGE (1991)

Caryl Phillips was born on the island of St Kitts in the West Indies in 1958 but moved to Britain with his family when he was still a baby, growing up in Leeds. He studied at Oxford and, after graduating, worked in the theatre. His first novel was published in 1985 and it has been followed by a very varied body of work that has ranged from further fiction to an anthology of writings on tennis, from TV scripts to books like *The Atlantic Sound* which fuse travel writing with historical and cultural meditation. Several of Phillips's novels are set in the Caribbean from which his family came and feature characters who struggle with the dark legacy of colonialism and the crises of identity that it can engender. *Cambridge* is a story which travels back into the past to deal overtly and directly with slavery and its terrible consequences. It uses two very different narrative voices – those of a nineteenth-century Englishwoman sent to visit her father's West Indies sugar plantation and of a gifted Christian slave, the eponymous Cambridge – to tell a chilling tale of an island society irredeemably tainted by the inhumanity on which it is built. Life on the plantation and the events which fuel the central plot are seen from the very different perspectives of the two narrators as the book moves towards a murder and a hanging which have the sombre inevitability of a Greek tragedy. Phillips has drawn upon the history of Atlantic slave trade and slavery in the Americas in novels he has published since *Cambridge*. *Crossing the River*, for example, begins with a father bewailing, 'I sold my beloved children' and opens out into a complex, intertwining narrative that shows how the legacy of that transaction between a destitute African and the master of an English slave ship echoes through two centuries of oppression. However, none of his other novels speaks to the reader of the terrible events of the past with quite the same moving directness as does the story of Cambridge.

☙ Read on

Crossing the River; *Dancing in the Dark* (a fictionalised version of the life of the black vaudeville performer Bert Williams); *The Nature of Blood*
Fred D'Aguiar, *Feeding the Ghosts*; Charles Johnson, *Middle Passage*

READ ON A THEME: BLACK HISTORY IN FICTION

David Dabydeen, *A Harlot's Progress*
Barbara Hambly, *A Free Man of Colour*
Lawrence Hill, *The Book of Negroes*
Toni Morrison, *A Mercy*
Walter Mosley, *Devil in a Blue Dress*
William Styron, *The Confessions of Nat Turner*
Margaret Walker, *Jubilee*

H.F.M. PRESCOTT (1896–1972) UK

THE MAN ON A DONKEY (1952)

The Man on a Donkey is not a book that would feature on everybody's list of the great works of the twentieth century. For long stretches of the five decades and more since it was published, it has been neglected and forgotten but it is a work of fiction that deserves far more attention and a wider readership than it has ever received. At the heart of this novel by Hilda Prescott is the popular protest in the north of England against Henry VIII's religious and social reforms which was known as the Pilgrimage of Grace. Through the stories of a small number of characters, from Robert Aske, the doomed leader of the rebellion against Henry's depredations, to a servant who has visions of Christ walking the land, she builds up a panoramic picture of one of the periods when the future of England hung in the balance. The struggle between conflicting visions of what the nation and the church should be ends at last in tragedy on a grand scale. Prescott was a scholar who was immersed in the details of Tudor history – her biography of Mary Tudor was long considered a definitive work – and her novel demonstrates her vast knowledge of the period. Yet the story she is telling never sinks beneath the weight of her erudition. Its historical detail is astonishing yet it always remains, first and foremost, a powerful tale of individuals caught up in the coils of great events. *The Man on a Donkey* is a remarkable work, a book which goes a long way towards justifying the words of one critic, writing in the 1970s when Prescott's magnum opus was actually out of print, who described it as 'the most distinguished historical novel in English in our time, and one of the most distinguished of any time'.

➬ Read on

Hella S. Haasse, *In a Dark Wood Wandering*; Zoe Oldenburg, *The World Is Not Enough*

STEVEN PRESSFIELD (b. 1943) USA

GATES OF FIRE (1998)

Steven Pressfield is a bestselling American author who has written a number of works of historical fiction about the military campaigns of the past, particularly those of the ancient world. *Gates of Fire*, his best-known novel, tells the story of Thermopylae, the legendary encounter in which a handful of Spartan warriors held at bay the might of the Persian Empire for days until they were betrayed, outflanked and finally slaughtered. The novel opens in the aftermath of the battle. The Spartans are dead but their courage has astonished the Persian king, Xerxes. He wants to know more about such men. A sole survivor has been dragged alive from the piles of Greek corpses. He is a squire named Xeones and it is his story, told to the king through interpreters, that forms Pressfield's narrative. Xeones is not himself a Spartan but a native of another Greek *polis* which was destroyed by its enemies when he was a boy. Orphaned and homeless as a consequence of his city's destruction, he makes his way to Sparta and becomes the servant of a warrior named Dienekes. Through Xeones's eyes, we see what makes Spartan society so different from those which surround it. We see, in brutally described detail, the relentless military training which every male Spartan must undergo. We witness the comradeship and devotion to ideas of honour and service to the state which emerge from that training. And, by the time Xeones follows Dienekes as the chosen warriors travel to make their heroic stand at Thermopylae, the Gates of Fire, we understand what it is that makes the Spartans the soldiers that they are. Pressfield succeeds brilliantly in evoking the horror and the violence of battle but his aim is to do more than that. Through the story of the three hundred at Thermopylae, he is looking to explore notions of courage, love and self-sacrifice that have permanent relevance and he does so in a novel that lingers long in the memory.

≋ Read on

Tides of War, *Last of the Amazons*

Conn Iggulden, *The Gates of Rome* (first of a sequence of novels based on the life of Julius Caesar); Ross Leckie, *Hannibal*; Valerio Massimo Manfredi, *The Spartan*; Scott Oden, *Memnon*

JULIAN RATHBONE (1935–2008) UK

THE LAST ENGLISH KING (1997)

For much of his forty-year literary career, Julian Rathbone was best-known as a writer of thrillers and crime stories, although he was twice shortlisted for the Booker Prize in the 1970s (once for a novel set in the past) and his greatest commercial success came in the last decade of his life with historical novels that made enjoyable use of deliberate anachronism and black humour. *Joseph*, the novel which reached the Booker shortlist in 1979, was a picaresque tale of a roguish con-artist on the loose in the Spain of the Peninsular War. Nearly twenty years later, Rathbone delved further back into the past to ask how the Battle of Hastings and the Norman Conquest appear to the defeated and the conquered. *The Last English King* opens a few years after the battle.

The focus of the narrative is Walt, only surviving member of King Harold's elite bodyguard. Scarred by defeat and guilty that he survived when worthier men did not, Walt has become a wanderer on the face of the earth. In Byzantium he meets up with a renegade monk named Quint and they embark on an eye-opening excursion through the eastern Mediterranean world as Walt undertakes a talking cure for his misery by telling his companion of the events that destroyed Anglo-Saxon England. Other books that took a tongue-in-cheek view of the past followed. *Kings of Albion* focuses on an unlikely band of visitors to an England torn apart by the Wars of the Roses. In *A Very English Agent* and *Birth of a Nation*, Rathbone returned to the central character from *Joseph* to have fun with the idea of a spy who may or may not be telling the truth about some of the great events of nineteenth-century history. Rackety and unreliable, the historical fiction Julian Rathbone wrote in the last ten years of his life was also brilliantly entertaining.

🕮 Read on

Birth of a Nation; *Kings of Albion*
>> Bernard Cornwell, *The Last Kingdom*; >> George MacDonald Fraser, *Black Ajax*

MARY RENAULT (1905–83) UK/SOUTH AFRICA

THE PRAISE SINGER (1978)

Mary Renault was born in London, educated at Oxford and was working as a nurse when her first novel, a romance with a contemporary setting, appeared in 1939. Other books followed, one of which won the MGM Award, a short-lived literary prize established by the film company in the 1940s as a means of unearthing novels worth turning into movies. Renault's novel never reached the screen but the money from MGM changed her life. She used it to move to South Africa which was her home for the rest of her life. She continued to write and turned to historical fiction in the 1950s. *The Last of the Wine*, the story of the intense relationship in peace and war between two young Athenian men, was the first of what were eventually eight novels set in ancient Greece. *The King Must Die* and *The Bull from the Sea* are based on the myth of Theseus who killed the Cretan Minotaur; *Fire from Heaven* is the first in a trilogy about Alexander the Great. *The Praise Singer* was written towards the end of Mary Renault's life and it contains all the storytelling verve and historical accuracy for which she was famous. The protagonist and narrator of the novel is a real-life historical individual – the lyric poet Simonides. Born on a small island in the Aegean, Simonides escapes the restricted destiny that seems most likely to be his when he is apprenticed to a travelling poet and singer who introduces him to the nomadic life he will lead for the rest of his days. Often admired but always an outsider wherever he goes, the poet is witness to the great events and personalities of the day and sees the first seeds of what will blossom into the Golden Age of Athens. Through the eyes of Simonides, Mary Renault gives readers one of her most vibrant and entrancing visions of the ancient world.

🕮 Read on

The Mask of Apollo; *Fire from Heaven*

>> Robert Graves, *Homer's Daughter*; >> Naomi Mitchison, *Cloud Cuckoo Land*; >> Rosemary Sutcliff, *The Flowers of Adonis*; Jill Paton Walsh, *Farewell, Great King*

READONATHEME: THE ANCIENT GREEKS

Gillian Bradshaw, *The Sun's Bride*

Lizabeth Cook, *Achilles*

Margaret Doody, *Aristotle Detective*

>> William Golding, *The Double Tongue*

Peter Green, *The Laughter of Aphrodite* (a story about the poet Sappho)

Tom Holt, *Goatsong*

Valerio Massimo Manfredi, *Alexander: Child of a Dream* (first in a trilogy about Alexander the Great)

Nicholas Nicastro, *The Isle of Stone*

H.N. Turteltaub, *Over the Wine-Dark Sea*

>> Barry Unsworth, *The Songs of the Kings*

DEREK ROBINSON (b. 1932) UK

GOSHAWK SQUADRON (1971)

Shortlisted for the Booker Prize in the year it was published, *Goshawk Squadron* was Derek Robinson's first novel. It is set in the last year of the First World War and follows the fortunes and (more often) misfortunes of a group of fighter pilots in the Royal Flying Corps. Some people may talk of the chivalry of the air and describe the pilots as modern versions of knights errant but, for Stanley Woolley, the prematurely cynical twenty-three year old who commands Goshawk Squadron, all such talk is nothing more than myth and propaganda. To Woolley, the purpose of the war is simple. His men are there to kill or be killed and, however successful an individual pilot may be in the aerial dogfights against the Germans, he's unlikely to survive more than three months. 'We eat death for breakfast,' he remarks memorably and the novel shows just how true his metaphor is. Since the publication of *Goshawk Squadron*, Robinson has gone on to produce a variety of other novels, most of them set in the past. *War Story* and *Hornet's Sting* are two further volumes which, together with his first novel, form a trilogy about the RFC in the First World War. He has also written a number of books set in the Second World War. *Kentucky Blues* marked a radical change in subject matter and is a kind of blackly comic western which takes place in Kentucky before and during the American Civil War. Sadly, since the book is very readable, Robinson has never returned to the West. However, of all the fiction he has produced in his career, *Goshawk Squadron* remains the best. At times reminiscent of Joseph Heller's *Catch-22* in its dark humour and its refusal to accept the comforting clichés of war, Robinson's debut novel is shocking, thrilling and intensely readable.

🐚 Read on
War Story; *Hornet's Sting*; *A Good Clean Fight* (set in the Second World War); *Kentucky Blues*
Alan Furst, *The World at Night*; Jack D. Hunter, *The Blue Max*

JANE ROGERS (b. 1952) UK

MR WROE'S VIRGINS (1991)

Jane Rogers has published seven novels since her first appeared in the early 1980s. Not all of them have been narratives set in the past but her best-known work, *Mr Wroe's Virgins*, is set in 1830s Lancashire. It tells the story of a charismatic, fire-and-brimstone preacher who seizes upon a Biblical text and uses it to persuade himself that God wishes him to live with seven virgins 'for comfort and succour'. When John Wroe announces this to his congregation, some of its members agree to submit to the demands of the Almighty and present him with their daughters. The events of the next nine months – before accusations of indecency and a scandalous trial bring the preacher's household to grief – are seen from the very different perspectives of four of the virgins. Each of the virgins has very different expectations of her place in the household and of what the future will bring. Leah is no virgin at all. She has secretly given birth to a son, the father has disappeared and her aim is to use her sexuality to attract Wroe's especial notice. Joanna is the most devout of the virgins, a woman for whom religion has become a repressive force, alienating her from self-knowledge. Hannah, intelligent and sceptical about all religious claims, has been led by accident and circumstance into the household. At first she is deeply resentful of Wroe and unimpressed by his status as an alleged visionary. She remains a sceptic but, ironically, it is Hannah in whom Wroe finds he can confide, and she finds herself drawn to him. The fourth 'virgin' is Martha, brutalised into a near animal existence by physical and sexual violence shown to her in the past. Through the different voices of the virgins, Rogers creates a poignant and intelligent novel which explores the mysteries of faith and love.

 Film version: *Mr Wroe's Virgins* (1993, TV miniseries, featuring Jonathan Pryce as Wroe)

 Read on
Promised Lands (two stories, one from the early years of Australia and one set in contemporary Britain, run in tandem)
Ronan Bennett, *Havoc, in its Third Year*; Michèle Roberts, *Fair Exchange*

RAFAEL SABATINI (1875–1950) ITALY/UK

CAPTAIN BLOOD (1922)

Rafael Sabatini published his first novels in the Edwardian era and he was still writing tales of derring-do in the late 1940s. Stories like *Scaramouche* and *Captain Blood* are best remembered in their film versions but his fiction can still be found in secondhand bookshops and on the web without much difficulty. Old-fashioned it may be but it still has an energy and readability that make it worth investigating. *Scaramouche*, whose central character is memorably described as 'born with a gift of laughter and a sense that the world was mad', is the story of a lawyer turned actor and duelling revolutionary during the French Revolution. *Captain Blood* tells the story of its eponymous hero, an Irish physician who, after an adventurous youth, has settled in the West Country. However, the year is 1685 and events do not allow Blood his peaceful retirement. When the Duke of Monmouth lands at Lyme Regis and launches his attempt to overthrow his uncle James II, Blood refuses to fight for the rebels but, after the Battle of Sedgemoor, he does use his medical skills to tend the wounded and the dying. For this he is condemned at the Bloody Assizes, presided over by the notorious Judge Jeffreys, and eventually transported to Barbados as an indentured labourer. Blood is not a man to remain enslaved for long and, during a Spanish raid on the island, he makes his escape. At the head of an intrepid band of former convicts he becomes a daring privateer, terrorising the enemies of England. After James II loses his throne in the Glorious Revolution, Blood wins a pardon from the new monarchs, William and Mary, and he leaves his privateer past behind him, even gaining the position of Governor of Jamaica. Blood's fictional adventures owe something to the real-life career of Sir Henry Morgan but Sabatini takes Morgan's exploits and refashions them into one of the most enjoyable of all swashbuckling yarns.

◾ **Film versions:** *Captain Blood* (1935, starring Errol Flynn as Blood)

📖 **Read on**
Captain Blood Returns; *The Sea Hawk*
Jeffery Farnol, *The Broad Highway*; A.E.W. Mason, *Fire Over England*; Stanley J. Weyman, *A Gentleman of France*

C.J. SANSOM (b. 1952) UK

DISSOLUTION (2003)

The most complex and intriguing character in historical crime fiction to appear in the last ten years is probably the hunchbacked Tudor lawyer, Matthew Shardlake. He is the creation of C J. Sansom and the novel that introduced him to readers was *Dissolution*, set in the year 1537. Henry VIII's Dissolution of the Monasteries has begun and Shardlake, a supporter of Henry's ruthless chief minister Thomas Cromwell, has been sent to Scarnsea monastery on the Sussex coast to investigate the brutal killing of one of Cromwell's commissioners. Robin Singleton was found in the monastic kitchens with his head severed from his body. At the same time a sacrilegious ritual, involving the slaughter of a black cockerel, appears to have taken place in the church. Accompanied by a young protégé named Mark Poer, Shardlake arrives at Scarnsea to question the monks. All have something to hide, from a sensitive and troubled homosexual to a converted Moor whose dark skin and exotic background others distrust. Over them all hangs the threat that the monastery might close and the largely privileged life they have known come to an end. As Shardlake investigates, more murders take place and the lawyer is forced to question everything he believes and holds most dear. The reform movement which Cromwell has led and in which Shardlake has invested so much, both intellectually and emotionally, is revealed as little more than a game of Machiavellian *realpolitik*. *Dissolution* makes clever use of the conventions of the classic English mystery and the enclosed community within which it takes place lends itself well to the kind of claustrophobic puzzle that characterises the genre but perhaps the most memorable element in the story is Shardlake himself. Outwardly self-confident and yet inwardly self-doubting, the lawyer is an entirely convincing figure around whom Sansom can build his Tudor world and the novels which have followed *Dissolution* have only served to enrich and expand the character.

⮐ Read on

Dark Fire; *Sovereign*; *Revelation* (the others in the Shardlake series); *Winter in Madrid* (set in Spain during the Second World War)
Ariana Franklin, *Mistress of the Art of Death*; Karen Maitland, *Company of Liars*

READONATHEME: TUDOR TALES

Anthony Burgess, *A Dead Man in Deptford* (Christopher Marlowe)
George Garrett, *Death of the Fox*
Margaret Irwin, *Young Bess* (first in a trilogy about Elizabeth I)
Faye Kellerman, *The Quality of Mercy*
Edward Marston, *The Queen's Head*
Rosalind Miles, *I, Elizabeth*
Robert Nye, *The Voyage of the Destiny* (Sir Walter Raleigh)
Sonia Overall, *A Likeness*
Jean Plaidy, *Murder Most Royal*

STEVEN SAYLOR (b. 1956) US

ROMAN BLOOD (1991)

Steven Saylor is the author of a series of novels in which the real history of the dying days of the Roman Republic is brilliantly entwined with the life of a fictional character. Saylor's creation, Gordianus the Finder ('the last honest man in Rome', as another character calls him), is a tough, unsentimental but sympathetic hero and we see him ageing and maturing as the series progresses and the dangerous politics of the period swirl around him, occasionally sweeping him up in conspiracy and murder. Based on a real case involving the Roman orator and politician Cicero, *Roman Blood* was the first in the Gordianus series to be published and it showed immediately Saylor's talent for blending real history with fictional mystery. The year is 80 BC and the up-and-coming Cicero hires Gordianus to investigate the background to a murder case in which he is defending a man charged with killing his father. Sextus Roscius is a wealthy country landowner who has moved to the city to enjoy the fruits of his riches and left the running of the farm to his son. When the older Roscius is murdered it is his son who appears to have the motivation and must face the court charged with the most heinous of crimes. As Gordianus digs deeper, however, he finds that the case has wider ramifications. Its tentacles spread far beyond the Roscius family and go to the very heart of the political corruption and infighting that are tearing the Republic apart. *Roman Blood* is only the first in a series that has seen Gordianus the Finder investigate mysteries from the Appian Way to ancient Marseilles but, on its own, it justifies the claim of one critic that Saylor 'evokes the ancient world more convincingly than any other writer of his generation'.

ꙮ Read on

Arms of Nemesis; *Catilina's Riddle*; *The Venus Throw* (although there are short stories set in the periods between the novels, these are the next three full-length books in the series)

Wallace Breem, *Eagle in the Snow*; John Maddox Roberts, *The King's Gambit*; David Wishart, *Ovid*

SIR WALTER SCOTT (1771–1832) UK

ROB ROY (1817)

If any writer could be said to have 'invented' the historical novel, it is Sir Walter Scott. His so-called Waverley novels, published between 1814 and 1831, were the bestsellers of their day and they more or less began the tradition of historical fiction which has continued to the present day. The themes and motifs of Scott's fiction, and very often the settings, became those of a new and powerful genre of writing. Enormously influential throughout Europe and America, they were imitated by many writers, from >> Dumas to Fenimore Cooper, and the novels were adapted into countless theatrical and operatic versions during the nineteenth century. The range of Scott's historical settings is more extensive than is sometimes acknowledged and he produced fiction which takes place in the English Middle Ages (*Ivanhoe*), medieval France (*Quentin Durward*), the Middle East of the Crusades (*The Talisman*), and even the eleventh-century Byzantine Empire (the slightly misleadingly titled *Count Robert of Paris*). However, most of the Waverley novels were excursions through Scottish history and, although not all the book is set in Scotland, one the most typical of these is *Rob Roy*. Scott's plot is simple enough. In the 1710s, Frank Osbaldistone, the son of an English merchant, and his villainous cousin Rashleigh are rivals for the hand of Diana Vernon. Rashleigh embezzles money and frames Osbaldistone. Osbaldistone escapes to the highlands of Scotland, where he seeks help from Rob Roy, a Scottish version of Robin Hood, an outlaw nobler than those who have outlawed him. As the Jacobite Rebellion of 1715 unfolds around them, the central characters struggle to work out their own destinies amidst the larger historical events in which they are all embroiled. *Rob Roy* was extremely popular at the time of its first publication and it remains today one of Scott's most fluent, enjoyable and readable books.

⮒ Read on

Heart of Midlothian; *Ivanhoe*

Honoré de Balzac, *The Chouans*; James Fenimore Cooper, *The Last of the Mohicans*; ⟩⟩ Alexandre Dumas, *The Black Tulip*; Edward Bulwer Lytton, *The Last of the Barons*

READONATHEME: SCOTLAND

Margaret Elphinstone, *Islanders*
Douglas Galbraith, *The Rising Sun*
Neil M. Gunn, *The Silver Darlings*
Anthony O'Neill, *The Lamplighter*
Janet Paisley, *White Rose Rebel*
James Robertson, *Joseph Knight*
Reay Tannahill, *A Dark and Distant Shore*
Nigel Tranter, *The Bruce Trilogy*

ANYA SETON (1904–90) USA

KATHERINE (1954)

Daughter of the well-known naturalist and writer Ernest Thompson Seton, Anya Seton was the author of a large number of historical romances, beginning with *My Theodosia*, published in 1941, a novel about the life of the daughter of the controversial American vice-president Aaron Burr. Seton's best-known book is *Katherine*. First published in the 1950s but still popular enough in 2003 to find a place on the BBC's Big Read survey of Britain's best-loved books, this tells the story of Katherine Swynford, mistress of John of Gaunt. The novel opens as the naïve Katherine de Roet leaves the convent where she has been educated and prepares to embark on life in the very different atmosphere of Edward III's court. She may be very young but she is also very beautiful and she attracts the attention of John of Gaunt, the son of the king. Their love cannot be consummated. He is married already and she is destined to wed a country knight named Hugh Swynford. Only when they have both grown older does their passion for one another ignite. Katherine becomes John's mistress and bears him a family out of wedlock. Throughout all the drama and danger of life in a medieval court, she remains by his side and eventually they are able to wed, legitimising their children. By the end of the novel, Katherine, the daughter of an obscure herald from Picardy, has become (although she can never know this) the ancestress of the Tudor kings of England. Anya Seton's dramatic story retains the popularity it has had since its first publication because of the skill with which she evokes the world her heroine enters and because Katherine herself remains such a powerful character. Readers, particularly female readers, continue to respond to Seton's portrait of a strong woman surviving and prospering in a court dominated by men.

🐚 Read on
Avalon; *Dragonwyck*
Margaret Campbell Barnes, *Brief Gaudy Hour*; Elizabeth Chadwick, *The Marsh King's Daughter*; ➤ Philippa Gregory, *The White Queen*; Jean Plaidy, *Madame Serpent*; Kathleen Winsor, *Forever Amber*

MICHAEL SHAARA (1928–88) USA

THE KILLER ANGELS (1974)
Born in New Jersey, the son of Italian immigrants, Michael Shaara served in the Korean War as a young man and then launched himself as a writer in the 1950s when he began to publish short stories in a wide range of magazines. His first novel, the story of a Korean War veteran, appeared in 1968 and he published several more before his death from a heart attack in 1988. By far the most admired and best known of these is *The Killer Angels*. Winner of the Pulitzer Prize for Fiction in 1975, the novel tells the story of the Battle of Gettysburg. Unlike many similar novels, Shaara's fiction takes few, if any, liberties with the facts. His characters are all real-life participants in the battle; there is none of his

own invention. The narrative follows the recorded action with great exactitude. In most editions of the book there are maps to assist readers in making sense of events. *The Killer Angels* opens with a Confederate spy, searching for the enemy and suddenly finding himself in a position where he can look down into a valley and see 'the whole vast army' of Union men below him. At times, Shaara follows the battle with the bird's-eye view of that spy. Through his narration, we see the large-scale movements of the opposing armies as they sweep across the Pennsylvania landscape. Yet, at other moments, the book records events from the viewpoints of the men embroiled in the dirt, danger and death of the battlefield. We see the heroism and suffering of the individual soldiers and the decisions forced upon weary commanders lost amidst the dust and swirl of the fighting. The American Civil War has provided the subject matter for a large library of fiction over the years but few of the books in that library have combined historical accuracy with storytelling skill in quite the same way as *The Killer Angels*.

📽 Film version: *Gettysburg* (1993)

🗣 Read on
» Thomas Keneally, *Confederates*; Jeff Shaara, *Gods and Generals*; Jeff Shaara, *The Last Full Measure* (two novels by Michael Shaara's son which provide a prequel and a sequel to *The Killer Angels*)

READ**ON**A**THEME:** THE AMERICAN CIVIL WAR

Russell Banks, *Cloudsplitter* (John Brown and the Harper's Ferry raid)

James Lee Burke, *White Doves at Morning*

>> Bernard Cornwell, *Rebel*

Shelby Foote, *Shiloh*

MacKinlay Kantor, *Andersonville*

Margaret Mitchell, *Gone with the Wind*

Philip Lee Williams, *A Distant Flame*

Daniel Woodrell, *Woe to Live On* (filmed by Ang Lee as *Ride with the Devil*)

Stephen Wright, *The Amalgamation Polka*

Marly Youmans, *The Wolf Pit*

JANE SMILEY (b. 1951) USA

THE ALL-TRUE TRAVELS AND ADVENTURES OF LIDIE NEWTON

Jane Smiley won the Pulitzer Prize for Fiction with her 1991 novel *A Thousand Acres*, an ingenious re-working of Shakespeare's *King Lear* in the setting of the farmlands of Iowa. She has published more than a dozen other works of fiction. *The Greenlanders* is an ambitious epic set in a Norse settlement in medieval Greenland, where families struggle to create a life for themselves amidst the threats posed both by nature and by their neighbours. However, the best of her historical fiction is a book that puts a very American subject at the centre of its narrative. *The All-True Travels and Adventures of Lidie Newton* takes place in the battleground between pro- and anti-slave factions that was Kansas in the 1850s. The idealistic settlers of Kansas Territory find that they have to face not only the belligerence of their pro-slave neighbours but the intransigence of a land that is far from being the one of milk and honey that they imagined. The women of the book face the challenges more realistically than the men. (Smiley's fiction is full of strong women who get on with the daily tasks of life while the men have a tendency to make fine speeches and adopt noble postures.) Yet even the likeable and resourceful heroine Lidie is caught up in forces she cannot understand. Her husband is killed by pro-slavers and her attempt to make a stand for his ideals (by helping in the escape of a slave) turns to tragedy. Like her character, Jane Smiley faces up to some of the most difficult issues in American history (violence, racism and the relationships between the sexes) and struggles to make sense of them. Her book is both the story of Lidie Newton's self-discovery, told in her own distinctive voice, and a convincing reconstruction of a period of dramatic change.

🕮 Read on

The Greenlanders

Jim Fergus, *One Thousand White Women*; Annie Proulx, *Accordion Crimes*

ROBERT LOUIS STEVENSON (1850–94) UK

KIDNAPPED (1886)

Kidnapped takes place in 1751. The Jacobite Rebellion and Bonnie Prince Charlie's first triumphal and then tragic progress through the Highlands are only six years in the past. Scotland is still a country in upheaval where dangers lurk and betrayal is a constant threat. Stevenson's hero is sixteen-year-old David Balfour who, after the death of his father, discovers that he has an uncle of whom he never previously knew and an ancestral home he has never before visited. His uncle, unfortunately, proves to be a villain who sees David as a threat and arranges to have the young man kidnapped, taken on a ship and despatched to the plantations in America as an indentured labourer. The wicked uncle's plans are only spoiled because the ship is involved in a collision at sea and a renegade Jacobite named Allan Breck is also hauled on board. David overhears the captain plotting to do away with his unwanted extra passenger and he joins forces with the belligerent Breck to confront the would-be murderers. Eventually, after the ship runs aground while trying to thread its way through the waters surrounding the Hebrides, its two unwilling passengers make their separate escapes. They meet up again in equally difficult circumstances when they are believed jointly responsible for the murder of Colin Campbell, known as 'The Red Fox', a hated government agent in the Highlands. Together, they have to evade the Redcoats searching for them and travel south to confront David's uncle. Stevenson's gifts as a writer of page-turning narrative are seen at their best in *Kidnapped* but the book is also a brilliant exploration of ideas of Scottish national character as embodied in the fiery and reckless Allan Breck and the canny and cautious David Balfour.

📑 **Film versions:** *Kidnapped* (1960, with Peter Finch as Allan Breck); *Kidnapped* (1971, with Michael Caine as Breck)

📚 **Read on**
Catriona (further adventures of David Balfour); *The Master of Ballantrae*; *Treasure Island*
≫ Sir Arthur Conan Doyle, *Micah Clarke*; ≫ George MacDonald Fraser, *The Candlemass Road*

PATRICK SÜSKIND (b. 1949) GERMANY

PERFUME (1985)
Perfume, originally written in German, was one of the great European bestsellers of the 1980s. Subtitled 'The Story of a Murderer', it is a novel that possesses elements of a number of fictional genres, including those of fantasy and crime fiction, but Patrick Süskind's careful reconstruction of the assorted eighteenth-century milieus in which its anti-hero operates means that it can readily take its place in any list of historical fiction. The central character of the book is Jean-Baptiste Grenouille, 'one of the most gifted and abominable personages in an

era that knew no lack of gifted and abominable personages' as his creator describes him. Grenouille is the world's only olfactory genius. From his birth, he has no bodily odour himself and he finds the aroma of others so offensive that he spends seven years living as a hermit to avoid it, but he develops a sense of smell that can distinguish between thousands and thousands of different scents and he can re-create them all whenever he wishes. In the course of the novel, he puts his extraordinary talents to perverse use as he embarks on a quest to create the perfect scent. Unfortunately his goal can be only achieved through the deaths of young women and Grenouille is launched on a career as a serial killer of beautiful virgins that takes him to the foot of the scaffold and beyond. In the quarter of a century since *Perfume* was published, Süskind has published little else (a couple of novellas, a handful of short stories and a collection of essays) and he remains something of a literary enigma, shunning publicity and refusing most requests for interviews. However, his one novel continues to fascinate new readers. Disturbing in its detached descriptions of its bizarre protagonist and his crimes, *Perfume* is a one-off, a weird amalgam of horror story and historical novel that is wholly original.

🖿 **Film version:** *Perfume* (2006)

🖥 **Read on**

Angela Carter, *Nights at the Circus*; Nicholas Griffin, *The House of Sight and Shadow*; Andrew Miller, *Ingenious Pain*; Patrick McGrath, *Martha Peake*

READ ON A THEME: EIGHTEENTH CENTURY ADVENTURES

Clare Clark, *The Nature of Monsters*
Sophie Gee, *The Scandal of the Season*
Janet Gleeson, *The Thief Taker*
›› Philippa Gregory, *A Respectable Trade*
Nicholas Griffin, *The Requiem Shark*
Ross King, *Domino*
Allen Kurzweil, *A Case of Curiosities*
Dacia Maraini, *The Silent Duchess*
Sena Jeter Naslund, *Abundance* (about Marie Antoinette)
Jean-Francois Parot, *The Chatelet Apprentice*
Elizabeth Redfern, *The Music of the Spheres*
William Makepeace Thackeray, *Barry Lyndon*

ROSEMARY SUTCLIFF (1920–92) UK

THE EAGLE OF THE NINTH (1954)

Rosemary Sutcliff's novel is based on an old legend about a Roman legion that marched northwards, beyond the walls that marked the boundaries of civilisation, and disappeared without trace. Her hero is Marcus Flavius Aquila, a young soldier who arrives in Britain a dozen years after the disappearance of the Ninth Legion. He has a particular interest in the lost legionaries because his father was one of them but he can do nothing to investigate his father's fate until he is injured in a frontier fight against rebellious Britons and forced to leave the army. While recuperating from his wounds he joins the household of his uncle who has settled in Britain and there he learns of the possibility that the standard of the Ninth – the Eagle – may be in the possession of a tribe in the north of Scotland. Once he has recovered, Marcus and Esca, a freed slave who has become his comrade, embark on a perilous mission to recover the Eagle. Travelling as an itinerant Greek oculist and his native assistant, they leave the safety of Romanised Britain behind them and venture into the tribal territories beyond Hadrian's Wall. They succeed in locating the Eagle which is being held as a trophy of war by one of the clans that destroyed the Ninth Legion in battle and must then work out how to steal it and transport it back south of the border. Modern historical research suggests that the story of the lost legion is based on a misinterpretation of the surviving evidence. The Ninth Legion, far from being destroyed in Britain, was still active in Germany some years after the events described in Sutcliff's novel. However, the new revelations of its fate do nothing to diminish her book. Rosemary Sutcliff was one of the most imaginative writers of historical fiction for children the twentieth century produced and *The Eagle of the Ninth* remains her finest novel.

🐚 Read on

The Silver Branch; *The Lantern Bearers*

Caroline Lawrence, *The Thieves of Ostia*; Geoffrey Trease, *Word to Caesar*

READONATHEME: HISTORICAL FICTION FOR CHILDREN (AND ADULTS)

Sally Gardner, *I, Coriander*
Leon Garfield, *Smith*
Jamila Gavin, *Coram Boy*
Julia Golding, *The Diamond of Drury Lane*
Cynthia Harnett, *The Wool-Pack*
Rudyard Kipling, *Puck of Pook's Hill*
Captain Marryat, *The Children of the New Forest*
Philip Pullman, *The Ruby in the Smoke*
Celia Rees, *Witch Child*
Geoffrey Trease, *Cue for Treason*
Mark Twain, *The Prince and the Pauper*

ANDREW TAYLOR (b. 1951) UK

THE AMERICAN BOY (2003)

The ten-year-old American boy who provides the title for this compelling story of sex, death and money in Regency London is named Edgar Allan Poe. Taylor takes some of the facts about Poe's real-life childhood experiences in England and weaves them into a page-turning work of fiction. Poe came to London with his guardians, the Allans, in

1815, when he was six years old, and he later spent some time at the Reverend John Bransby's school in Stoke Newington. The narrator of Taylor's book (and a wholly invented character) is Thomas Shield, a teacher at the school. Shield is a man with an unhappy past. He fought at the Battle of Waterloo and his military service has scarred him psychologically. While working for Bransby, Shield is introduced to the family of Charles Frant, another boy at the school and a playfellow of the young Poe. Before long, he is drawn into the web of intrigue that surrounds the Frants. The father appears to become the victim of a brutal murder. The schoolmaster, appointed tutor to young Frant and his American friend, is strongly attracted to the newly widowed mother but he can do little to express his desires because of the difference in their social status. Meanwhile, a shady character who may or may not be Edgar Allan's missing father is lurking in the background. As the plot becomes ever more entangled, Shield enters a world where nothing is quite as it seems and the greedy and the corrupt hold all the power. Andrew Taylor has been one of the most consistently interesting writers of thrillers and crime fiction in the last twenty years. Until the publication of *The American Boy*, he was probably best known for the 'Roth Trilogy', a sequence of novels which delves deeper and deeper into the past life of a psychopathic killer. His reconstruction of the Regency world which shaped the imagination of Edgar Allan Poe revealed him as a master of the historical mystery novel.

🐃 Read on
Bleeding Heart Square
Louis Bayard, *The Pale Blue Eye*; James Bradley, *The Resurrectionist*

READ ON A THEME: WRITERS' LIVES

Novels featuring famous writers

Julian Barnes, *Arthur & George* (Sir Arthur Conan Doyle)

Anthony Burgess, *Nothing Like the Sun* (William Shakespeare)

Frederick Busch, *The Night Inspector* (Herman Melville)

›› Tracy Chevalier, *Burning Bright* (William Blake)

J.M. Coetzee, *The Master of Petersburg* (Fyodor Dostoevsky)

Michael Dibdin, *A Rich Full Death* (Robert Browning)

Helen Dunmore, *Counting the Stars* (Catullus)

Carlos Fuentes, *The Old Gringo* (Ambrose Bierce)

Tom Holland, *The Vampyre* (Lord Byron as one of the undead)

Michèle Roberts, *Fair Exchange* (William Wordsworth)

›› Steven Saylor, *A Twist at the End* (O. Henry)

C.K. Stead, *Mansfield* (Katherine Mansfield)

Colm Toibin, *The Master* (Henry James)

ADAM THORPE (b. 1956) UK

ULVERTON (1992)

Adam Thorpe began his writing career as a poet and he continues to publish regular collections of his verse. His fiction shows a poet's sensitivity to the smaller subtleties and nuances of language but it has also demonstrated an ambition to tell stories on a grand scale. *Ulverton* was his first novel. In it Thorpe creates an imaginary West Country village which provides the book with a title and then, in twelve very different narratives, he peoples it with individuals from several centuries of its history. 'Friends', set in 1689, is ostensibly a sermon by the Reverend Mr Brazier to his congregation but manages also to be an account of individual tragedies (the deaths of two men in a snowstorm) and a snapshot of English religion caught between established Anglicanism and the increasingly powerful forces of Dissent. In 'Deposition', set in 1830, Thorpe encapsulates the class tensions of the time in a story of rioting, machine-breaking and the unbridgeable gulf between Ulverton's squire, with his desire to carve a White Horse in a chalky hillside near the village, and impoverished villagers with nothing but contempt for his well-meaning scheme. Each chapter works as an individual story but they weave together to form the longer story of Ulverton across three hundred years. The reader is shown the change and the continuity in one English community as it is shaped by time. The book ends in 1988 with a piece that takes the form of the script for a TV documentary about a greedy and unimaginative property developer on a collision course with conservationists. Ulverton is a bravura performance, in which Thorpe recreates and re-imagines the voices of the past. It is a demanding, sometimes difficult read but a very rewarding one.

🕮 Read on
Nineteen Twenty One; *Hodd* (Thorpe's version of the Robin Hood stories)

ROSE TREMAIN (b. 1943) UK

RESTORATION (1989)
Rose Tremain published her first novel in 1976 and was one of Granta's 20 Best of Young British Writers in 1983 but it was only with the publication of *Restoration* that she began to attract the kind of wider attention and readership her talent deserved. The book tells the story of Robert Merivel, a minor courtier attendant on Charles II. Merivel is a physician who first attracts the king's attention when he saves the life of one Charles's much-loved dogs and is promptly given the job of tending to the rest of them. At first caught up in the amoral hedonism of the court, Merivel is later paired off in a marriage of convenience with Celia Clemence, one of Charles's mistresses, and given an estate in Norfolk to console him for the fact that his new wife, in reality, belongs to the king. When he has the temerity to make advances to Celia, he falls from grace with the king and is obliged to make his way in the

world without his favour. He goes to live with a Quaker friend from college who runs a madhouse in East Anglia but his attempt to recover his vocation as a healer also ends in disaster. It is only when he is back in London at the time of the Plague and the Great Fire that he succeeds, as much by accident as design, in restoring himself to the king's favours. A portrait of a man torn between the physical and the spiritual, between his desire to indulge himself in all of the many pleasures available to him at certain points in his life and his nagging sense that they are essentially meaningless, *Restoration* is a wonderfully vigorous reconstruction of the age of contradictions in which it is set. Tremain has written other historical novels, most notably *Music and Silence* which follows the career of an English lutenist at the court of Christian IV, a seventeenth-century king of Denmark, but *Restoration* is the book that remains her most compelling and engaging excursion into the past.

Film version: *Restoration* (1993, with Robert Downey Jr as Merivel)

Read on
The Colour; *Music and Silence*
Rose Macaulay, *They Were Defeated*; Maria McCann, *As Meat Loves Salt*; Jane Stevenson, *Astraea*

BARRY UNSWORTH (b. 1930) UK

MORALITY PLAY (1995)

Barry Unsworth has been publishing critically acclaimed fiction since the 1960s and much of his work has been set in the past. *Pascali's Island*, for example, set on an Aegean island during the dying days of the Ottoman Empire, records the dance of deception between a Turkish spy and a visiting English archaeologist. *Sacred Hunger*, which was joint winner of the Booker Prize in 1992, is a powerful narrative of the eighteenth-century Atlantic slave trade. *The Ruby in her Navel* is set in the multi-cultural melting pot that was twelfth-century Norman Sicily. All of Unsworth's historical novels are worth reading but one of the most effective and unusual is the medieval murder mystery, *Morality Play*. This novel's central character, Nicholas Barber, is a priest who is bored and restless in the Church and escapes to join a group of travelling players. Plague, physical and spiritual, affects the land. The troupe arrives in a town where a murder has taken place and a woman has been condemned for it. Despairing of an audience for their conventional biblical dramas, the players take the radical step of re-enacting the murder and the events surrounding it. Not only is this unprecedented aesthetically ('Who plays things that are done in the world?', one of the actors demands) but, when the re-enactment threatens to reveal new truths about the crime, it puts the players into physical danger. The murderer is not the woman about to hang. The real murderer is still at large to put into jeopardy those who could demonstrate the truth. *Morality Play*, a story that combines elements of a murder mystery and a fable about art and meaning, reveals the immediacy with which Unsworth can thrust his readers back into a richly imagined past.

◀ **Film version:** *The Reckoning* (2003)

🕮 **Read on**
Pascali's Island; *The Ruby in her Navel*; *Sacred Hunger*

GUY VANDERHAEGHE (b. 1951) CANADA

THE LAST CROSSING (2001)

The North American West in 1871 is no place for an English gentleman and saintly Simon Gaunt, would-be missionary, has discovered this the hard way. He has disappeared while taking the word of God to the Indians and his two brothers travel from England to enter the wilderness in search of him. His twin Charles is a painter, defying the wishes of his tyrannical father to pursue his artistic vocation; older brother Addington is a preening, self-satisfied egotist who dreams of the heroic figure he will cut as a big-game hunter and of the book that will be written about his exploits. Guided by an enigmatic half-breed, Jerry Potts, and accompanied by a troubled civil-war veteran, a woman intent on tracking down her sister's murderers and a garrulous journalist, the two men stumble towards the astonishing truth about their brother's fate. Told from the viewpoints of several different characters, *The Last Crossing* is a rich novel in which traditional themes of the western are given a new vitality and power. Its author is a Canadian, Guy Vanderhaeghe, who was born and brought up in

Saskatchewan and began writing in the 1970s. His first book of short stories won the Governor General's Award for Fiction, Canada's most prestigious literary prizes, in 1982. His first novel followed two years later but Vanderhaeghe was little known outside Canada until the appearance of *The Englishman's Boy* in 1996. A story which links Hollywood in the 1920s to one of the most infamous events in the real-life history of the Canadian West, the so-called Cypress Hills Massacre, it was published around the world and won much critical praise. Five years later, *The Last Crossing* appeared and gained similar accolades. Both books can readily take their places in any list of the best historical fiction of the last twenty years.

🍃 **Read on**
The Englishman's Boy
Gil Adamson, *The Outlander*; Stef Penney, *The Tenderness of Wolves*

GORE VIDAL (b. 1925) USA

BURR (1973)
Gore Vidal is now one of the grand old men of American literature. Since his debut novel *Williwaw*, a story of the war in the Pacific written when he was still in his teens, he has published more than twenty novels and also produced screenplays, detective stories, political polemics and some of the best American essays of the last hundred years. All of his

fiction is original and stimulating but his historical novels have a particular power to seize the reader's imagination. He has written of the ancient world with tremendous vitality and vividness. *Julian* is a study of the last pagan Roman emperor, who tried to stop the rush of Christianity in the name of (as Vidal sees it) the more humane, more generous Olympian religion. *Creation* is the memoirs of an imaginary Persian nobleman of the fifth century BC, who went as ambassador to India, China and Greece and knew Confucius, Buddha and Socrates. However, his finest achievement in fiction is his long, interconnected sequence of novels about the rise to great power status of his native land. The first of these is *Burr* which tells the story of Aaron Burr, third vice-president of the USA and one of the more colourful politicians from the early years of the new nation. Vidal has always prided himself on his iconoclasm, and his refusal to accept what he sees as comforting myths about America's past, and *Burr* provides an unsurprisingly idiosyncratic view of the Revolutionary era. George Washington is less national hero or military genius and more opportunist politician; Thomas Jefferson is an idol with feet of clay. However, the focus of the book is firmly on Burr, seen through the eyes of a later journalist investigating his career and (in an imagined memoir) through his own. He is a fascinating character and, in Vidal's hands, the story of his rise and spectacular fall presents a new perspective on the founding of a nation.

☙ Read on

Lincoln; *1876* (and the further four books in the 'Narratives of Empire' sequence); *Creation*

LEW WALLACE (1827–1905) USA

BEN-HUR (1880)

Lewis Wallace has a number of claims to fame. To students of the American Civil War, he is known as the Union general who played a controversial role in the Battle of Shiloh, one of the most significant engagements of the war. By historians of the Wild West, he is best remembered as the Governor of New Mexico who once met with Billy the Kid and offered him an amnesty. However, he is most widely known as the author of *Ben-Hur*, one of the bestselling American novels of the nineteenth century and a book that has never been out of print in all the years since its first publication. Much of the book's success stems from its combination of adventure fiction with Christian piety. The central character of the book is Judah ben Hur, a prince from the royal family of Judaea, who grows up in Jerusalem at the time of Christ. Wrongly accused of attempting to kill the Roman governor of Judaea and betrayed by his childhood friend Messala, he is sent into slavery and a life chained to the oars of a Roman warship. Fate takes a hand when Ben-Hur saves the life of a wealthy Roman citizen during a shipwreck and the Roman, in gratitude, adopts him. Ben-Hur himself becomes a Roman citizen and eventually inherits his benefactor's wealth. He returns to his homeland to discover what happened to his family and to pursue vengeance against Messala. Throughout the book, the hero's trials and tribulations are intertwined with the life of Jesus. At crucial moments in the story Ben-Hur encounters Christ and the novel culminates in the crucifixion and his realisation that the man he thought might prove an earthly king is, in truth, a heavenly saviour. Most people now know the story of Judah ben Hur only through the

1950s film version starring Charlton Heston in the lead role. The book on which the film was based still deserves to be read.

🎬 **Film version:** *Ben-Hur* (1959, starring Charlton Heston in the title role)

📖 **Read on**
Lloyd C. Douglas, *The Robe*; Henryk Sienkiewicz, *Quo Vadis*

MIKA WALTARI (1908–79) FINLAND

THE EGYPTIAN (1945/1949)

In his native Finland Mika Waltari is considered one of the great writers of the twentieth century and much of his work can be classified as historical fiction. *The Adventurer* and *The Wanderer*, two novels which tell the story of a footloose young man roaming sixteenth-century Europe and the Middle East, *The Dark Angel*, set at the time of the Fall of Constantinople, and *The Secret of the Kingdom*, about a Roman citizen who becomes an early Christian in Jerusalem, are all books which remain worth reading. However, Waltari's magnum opus is undoubtedly *The Egyptian*, published in Finnish in 1945 and in English four years later. It became a huge international success, selling more copies in America than any other novel in translation before ›› Umberto

Eco's *The Name of the Rose* and it was made into a Hollywood epic in the 1950s. Its fame has faded in recent decades but it is still in print and it remains a powerful work of historical imagination. It is set in one of the most tumultuous periods in the history of ancient Egypt and during the reign of Akhenaten, one of its most controversial pharaohs. Its central character is Sinuhe (Waltari took the name from a well-known ancient Egyptian text), a man who has once been physician to the pharaoh. From exile he tells the story of his life. 'I write not to glorify the gods, for I am weary of gods,' he tells readers. 'I write not to glorify pharaohs, for I am weary of pharaohs' deeds. Rather for my own sake do I write this.' Through the eyes of Sinuhe, readers get a highly-coloured reconstruction of an era of change and upheaval (Waltari's descriptions of the sex lives of the Ancient Egyptians, tame enough today, were considered particularly racy at the time of first publication) and of one man's search for meaning amidst apparent chaos.

🎬 **Film version:** *The Egyptian* (1954)

📖 **Read on**
The Adventurer; *The Wanderer*; *The Dark Angel*; *The Etruscan*; *The Secret of the Kingdom*

READ ON A THEME: ANCIENT EGYPT

Agatha Christie, *Death Comes as the End* (in one of her very
  few ventures into historical mysteries, the Queen of Crime
  tells the story of a serial killer in Ancient Egypt)
P.C. Doherty, *The Mask of Ra*
Anton Gill, *City of the Dead*
H. Rider Haggard, *Cleopatra*
Lauren Haney, *The Right Hand of Amon*
Christian Jacq, *The Son of the Light*
Naguib Mahfouz, *Akhenaten, Dweller in Truth*
Norman Mailer, *Ancient Evenings* (Mailer's own very
  idiosyncratic take on Egypt in the reign of Ramses the Great)
Wilbur Smith, *River God*
Duncan Sprott, *The House of the Eagle* (the first volume in
  what will eventually be a four-volume sequence about the
  Ptolemies)

SARAH WATERS (b. 1966) UK

FINGERSMITH (2002)

Sarah Waters has written some of the most adventurous and original historical fiction of the last decade. Her first three novels, all set in the Victorian era, took many of the themes and motifs of the literature of the period and put them to new uses, creating characters and settings that her nineteenth-century predecessors firmly excluded from their fiction. In *Tipping the Velvet* central character Nan Astley is drawn into new experiences when she meets male impersonator Kitty Butler. Nan's picaresque adventures in the hidden lesbian sub-culture of Victorian London constitute a riotous voyage of self-discovery through a world of rowdy music hall entertainers, Sapphic aristos with a taste for working-class girls and cross-dressing gender-benders. Sarah Waters's second novel, *Affinity*, is a dark tale of nineteenth-century spiritualism and eroticism that focuses on the relationship between a repressed, upper middle-class spinster and a supposed medium imprisoned for fraud. *Fingersmith* was Waters's third fictional excursion into the sexual and social sub-cultures of the Victorian era and, in many ways, her best. It opens in the thieves' dens of 1860s Southwark and expands into an elaborate story of cross and double-cross centred on a suave con-man's attempt to use the heroine, Susan Trinder, in his plot to defraud a wealthy heiress. Little is what it seems as Susan and her intended victim, Maud Lilly, develop an intimacy that threatens to shipwreck the schemes of all the main characters. Told in the narrative voices of Susan and Maud, each one revealing a little more of the truth to the reader, the book takes many of the characters and motifs of Victorian melodrama (the moustache-twirling villain, the innocent orphan, the ever-present threat of the madhouse or the workhouse) and gives them new life. *Fingersmith*, like Sarah Waters's first two books, plays knowing and sophisticated games with readers' expectations of a Victorian novel but also provides a story which possesses its own ability to grip the imagination.

📥 **Film version:** *Fingersmith* (2005, TV film)

📖 **Read on**
Affinity; *Tipping the Velvet*
Jane Harris, *The Observations*; Sylvia Townsend Warner, *Summer Will Show*

PATRICK WHITE (1912–90) AUSTRALIA

VOSS (1957)

In 1857, a group of explorers sets out to cross Australia. The expedition is led by Johann Ulrich Voss, a German visionary based on the real-life explorer Ludwig Leichhardt who disappeared in the outback in the 1840s. The other members include an ex-convict and a dreamy Aboriginal boy, Jackie, torn between the white people's culture and his own. White balances reports of the expedition's struggle against the desert and to understand one another with accounts of the life of Laura Trevelyan, a young woman fascinated by Voss (at first as an epic personality and then as a vulnerable human being) as she waits in Sydney for news of him. As difficulty mounts upon difficulty and the expedition is increasingly threatened by the unforgiving landscape they have entered, Voss's sense of self begins to fracture and disintegrate. Patrick White was one of the greatest writers Australia has produced – he remains the only Australian to have won the Nobel Prize for Literature – and his fiction has a grandeur and an ambition that few others can match. A number of his novels have looked back into Australia's past for their inspiration. *A Fringe of Leaves*, for example, is the story of a woman shipwrecked in Queensland in the 1840s, who is captured by Aborigines and forced to re-think her ideas about 'civilisation' and 'savagery'. However, none of his other historical narratives can match his tale of the nineteenth-century explorer. Voss's journey into a physical and spiritual wilderness is described with vivid intensity and his mystical connection with Laura, which only deepens as the distance between them increases, is presented with a power that transcends any doubts the reader might have about the possibility of its existing. Voss himself becomes a figure of almost mythical proportions. *Voss* is not an easy or a comforting read. It demands commitment and attention but, if the reader perseveres, it provides its own particular and substantial rewards.

📚 Read on

A Fringe of Leaves
André Brink, *An Instant in the Wind*; David Malouf, *Remembering Babylon*

READ**READ**ON**A**THEME: EXPLORING THE WORLD

>> Beryl Bainbridge, *The Birthday Boys*
   George Mackay Brown, *Vinland*
>> Robert Edric, *The Broken Lands*
   Stephen Marlowe, *The Memoirs of Christopher Columbus*
   Roger McDonald, *Mr Darwin's Shooter*

MARGUERITE YOURCENAR (1903–87)
BELGIUM/FRANCE

MEMOIRS OF HADRIAN (1951)

One of the most widely respected French writers of the twentieth century and the first woman ever to be elected a member of the prestigious Académie Française, Marguerite Yourcenar published her first book in the 1920s and continued to produce poetry, fiction, essays and memoirs until her death sixty years later. Her best-known book, *Memoirs of Hadrian*, is based on the life of the second-century Roman emperor. The real Hadrian did indeed write a memoir (since lost) but it is safe to assume that it was very different from Yourcenar's book which takes the form of a long letter by the emperor, addressed to his distant kinsman and eventual successor Marcus Aurelius. When the novel opens, the ageing Hadrian has just returned from a chastening visit to his physician and he is forced to contemplate his body's decline and the end that awaits emperors as inevitably as it does common men. His response is to provide a testament for the man who will take his place, recounting his life from his early years to his years of power. Yourcenar's portrait of Hadrian draws on a deep knowledge of the Roman Empire but it is the psychological insight rather than the historical accuracy of the book that is most striking. Great events happen throughout the novel – these are after all the memoirs of the most powerful man in the world – but they take second place to the impact they have on Hadrian and the development of his self. We see the emperor as thinker and lover (his impassioned, obsessive relationship with the young man Antinous is central to the book) as much as, if not more than, we see him as ruler and soldier. Melancholic and moving, Yourcenar's imagined imperial memoirs come together in one of the great French novels of the twentieth century.

🕮 Read on

The Abyss (set in Renaissance Flanders)
Gabriel Garcia Marquez, *The General in his Labyrinth* (a very different setting – South America – and a very different protagonist – Simon Bolivar – but another book in which a powerful ruler reflects on his past); Thornton Wilder, *The Ides of March*; John Williams, *Augustus*

RICHARD ZIMLER (b. 1956) USA

THE LAST KABBALIST OF LISBON (1998)

Born in New York, Richard Zimler moved to Portugal in 1990 and still lives and works there. He now has dual American and Portuguese nationality. Much of his fiction draws upon the history of his adopted country and his best-known books form an interconnected sequence of stories, known as the 'Sephardic Cycle' about different branches and generations of a Portuguese Jewish family. In *The Last Kabbalist of Lisbon*, a renowned scholar is murdered during an anti-Jewish pogrom in early sixteenth-century Lisbon and his nephew devotes himself to tracking down the killer. Berekiah Zarco is a young manuscript illuminator in the city who, like many of his people at the time, is leading a double life. Outwardly he is one of the converted Jews known as 'New Christians' but he also remains committed to his Jewish past and, in particular, to the mystical tradition known as the kabbala. Lisbon is in turmoil and 'Old Christians' blame 'New Christians' for its troubles. Riots erupt in the city streets and, amidst the violence, the motives for one death can be hidden. When the body of Berekiah's uncle and mentor, Abraham, is found in his scriptorium in particularly degrading circumstances, the young man vows to find those responsible. Told in the words of Berekiah himself in a memoir supposedly written after he has escaped from Portugal and unearthed centuries after his death, *The Last Kabbalist of Lisbon* shows its protagonist embarking on a journey through the dangerous labyrinth of the city's religious politics in his attempts to learn the truth. What he finds as he and his close friend, a young deaf-mute Muslim named Farid, pursue their investigations goes to the very heart of the Christian persecution of Jews in Lisbon. Zimler cleverly combines elements of an historical mystery novel with a devastating portrait of a city falling prey to prejudice and pogrom.

📖 Read on

Hunting Midnight; *Guardian of the Dawn*; *The Seventh Gate*
Miguel Delibes, *The Heretic*; David Liss, *A Conspiracy of Paper*; Peter Prince, *Adam Runaway*

INDEX